The
PROOF

ALSO BY JAMES F. TWYMAN

BOOKS

The Art of Spiritual Peacemaking
The Barn Dance*
Emissary of Light
Emissary of Love
The Kabbalah Code*
Messages from Thomas
The Moses Code*
The Prayer of St. Francis
Praying Peace
The Proposing Tree
The Secret of the Beloved Disciple
Ten Spiritual Lessons I Learned at the Mall

FILMS

Indigo
The Indigo Evolution
Into Me See
The Moses Code: The Movie*
The Proof

MUSIC

Ecclesia
Emissary of Light
For the Beloved
God Has No Religion
May Peace Prevail on Earth
The Moses Code Frequency Meditation*
The Order of the Beloved Disciple

*Available from Hay House

Please visit Hay House USA: **www.hayhouse.com**®
Hay House Australia: **www.hayhouse.com.au**
Hay House UK: **www.hayhouse.co.uk**
Hay House South Africa: **www.hayhouse.co.za**
Hay House India: **www.hayhouse.co.in**

The PROOF

**A 40-Day Program
for Embodying Oneness**

JAMES F. TWYMAN

with Anakha Coman

HAY HOUSE, INC.
Carlsbad, California • New York City
London • Sydney • Johannesburg
Vancouver • Hong Kong • New Delhi

Published and distributed in the United States by: Hay House, Inc.: www.hayhouse
.com • *Published and distributed in Australia by:* Hay House Australia Pty. Ltd.:
www.hayhouse.com.au • *Published and distributed in the United Kingdom by:*
Hay House UK, Ltd.: www.hayhouse.co.uk • *Published and distributed in the
Republic of South Africa by:* Hay House SA (Pty), Ltd.: www.hayhouse.co.za •
Distributed in Canada by: Raincoast: www.raincoast.com • *Published in India
by:* Hay House Publishers India: www.hayhouse.co.in

Editorial supervision: Jill Kramer • *Design:* Tricia Breidenthal

Library of Congress Cataloging-in-Publication Data

Twyman, James F.
 The proof : a 40-day program for embodying oneness / James F. Twyman, with
Anakha Coman. -- 1st ed.
  p. cm.
 ISBN 978-1-4019-2640-3 (hardcover : alk. paper) 1. Spiritual life. 2. Self-
realization. I. Coman, Anakha. II. Title.
 BL624.T93 2009
 299'.93--dc22

                                    2009015133

Tradepaper ISBN: 978-1-4019-2641-0

13 12 11 10 6 5 4 3
1st edition, October 2009
3rd edition, October 2010

Printed in the United States of America

*To Chuck Anderson, the
One who opened the Door.*

— James Twyman

*To Yeshua, my constant companion;
and to Andrew Harvey, for his
exquisite guidance on this journey
home to the sacred heart.*

— Anakha Coman

≈ CONTENTS ≈

Preface ix
A Beginning xiii

PART I: The 40-Day Oneness Program 1

The First 20 Practices: A Place to Begin 5

Practice 1:   The Rhythm of Oneness 7
Practice 2:   The Breath of Oneness 11
Practice 3:   The Sound of Oneness 15
Practice 4:   The Gaze of Oneness 20
Practice 5:   The Heart of Oneness 24
Practice 6:   The Body of Oneness 29
Practice 7:   The Restoration of Oneness 33
Practice 8:   The Source of Oneness 37
Practice 9:   The Belonging of Oneness 41
Practice 10:   The Soul of Oneness 45
Practice 11:   The Embrace of Oneness 49
Practice 12:   The Temple of Oneness 54
Practice 13:   The Elixir of Oneness 58
Practice 14:   The Sensation of Oneness 63
Practice 15:   The Touch of Oneness 68
Practice 16:   The Seeds of Oneness 72
Practice 17:   The Blossoming of Oneness 77
Practice 18:   The Creativity of Oneness 81
Practice 19:   The Spontaneity of Oneness 86
Practice 20:   The Desire of Oneness 91

Dialogue on Practices 21–30 97

Practice 21: The Shadow of Oneness 99
Practice 22: The Fear of Oneness 104
Practice 23: The Heartbreak of Oneness 109
Practice 24: The Grievance of Oneness 113
Practice 25: The Crucible of Oneness 118
Practice 26: The Fire of Oneness 123
Practice 27: The Reconciliation of Oneness 128
Practice 28: The Forgiveness of Oneness 133
Practice 29: The Humility of Oneness 138
Practice 30: The Endurance of Oneness 142

Introduction to Practices 31–40 147

Practice 31: The Communion of Oneness 149
Practice 32: The Community of Oneness 153
Practice 33: The Discipleship of Oneness 158
Practice 34: The Vision of Oneness 162
Practice 35: The Ministry of Oneness 167
Practice 36: The Kingdom of Oneness 171
Practice 37: The Intimacy of Oneness 175
Practice 38: The Prayer of Oneness 181
Practice 39: The Journey of Oneness 185
Practice 40: The Mystery of Oneness 190

PART II: Achieving the Impossible 197

Lesson 1: The Sense of Touch 201
Lesson 2: The Language Beneath All Language 211
Lesson 3: The Final Step 217

Afterword 221
About the Authors 225

⤜ PREFACE ⤏

On April 15, 2009, I released a 20-minute film on the Internet called *The Proof*. It's the fifth work that I've either directed or produced, and it's my first short film. The first one I helped create was a movie called *Indigo,* which enjoyed incredible success. Acclaimed producer and director Stephen Simon, best-selling author Neale Donald Walsch, and I pioneered a new way of producing and distributing spiritually minded films—something that Stephen called "spiritual cinema." Other films followed, and we released them through an intricate network of hundreds of churches, organizations, and independent theaters around the world. However, *The Proof* was meant to be different. I wanted people to be able to see it for free, and I also wanted to attempt something that no one had ever done before. It would be a tricky balance, but I decided to give myself to it and see where it might lead.

The deeper meaning behind the concept of *Oneness* has been steadily simmering on the back burner of my mind for quite some time, and it brings me great joy to finally express what I've learned over the years in an inspiring film (and now this book). But in order to truly understand this wisdom, you need to know how my own search for *the proof* began.

When I was 17, I discovered something that changed my life. I've always been interested in the occult and was visiting a magic shop when I came across a little booklet called *Hellstromism*. I think I was attracted to the mysterious title more than anything else, and I couldn't wait to get home to see what it offered. The book detailed a unique form of mentalism that had been developed by a man named Alex Hellstrom in the early 20th century. He realized that when a person thinks about something, there are very subtle physical reactions that accompany the thought, which can be picked up by those who are acutely perceptive. Hellstrom made a career out of performing this "magic" by having people hide objects in theaters and other places; and then seemingly reading their minds, he'd locate the hidden items. He referred to this remarkable skill as *muscle reading,* and it's still practiced today.

I was fascinated and swallowed it down like it was the elixir of life itself. Before long, I'd mastered the technique and began demonstrating my skills to anyone who would watch. Unfortunately for my family, they became my first audience members and had to endure my ceaseless practicing; then throughout college, I continued to perfect my technique. In the end, it was nothing more than a good party trick, but I enjoyed it immensely.

It was only a few years ago when I noticed that something had changed. As I opened myself up spiritually over the years, I became more sensitive to the subtle vibrations that had no real physical counterparts. Simply put, I realized that I could actually read the energy a person emitted. I couldn't do it every time—in fact, my success rate was at about 40 percent, but it was enough to show me that I'd jumped to a new level. It suddenly stopped being a "trick" and was now something very different and new: I was experiencing what some people might refer to as *mind reading.*

Then one day I had a thought: it wasn't that I was reading people's minds, but that I was somehow bypassing the idea of separation, experiencing myself as *one* with them. I started noticing this in many other areas of my life, too. There were prolonged periods when I couldn't tell where a particular person stopped and I began. It was a phenomenon that I had read about in the lives of the greatest mystics and saints, and now it was happening to *me.*

The idea to make *The Proof* film seemed like a fun way to begin the conversation. I decided to ask someone to hide a book anywhere in the United States, and then I'd attempt to find it with only the aid of my trusty volunteer *thinking* about the location. I'd heard about people using Hellstromism to locate objects hidden in a city or town, but no one had the guts to try this. It sounded crazy at first, but the more I thought about it the more I realized that I could do it. In fact, Reid Tracy, the president of Hay House (my publisher), decided to engage in a bet: if I found the hidden book, Hay House would donate $50,000 to the Louise Hay Foundation. If I didn't, then *I* had to make the donation myself. I immediately began practicing at the local mall with amazing success. Eventually, it was time to go for broke—literally—and the film is the story of that experience.

I didn't set out to conduct a scientific experiment with double-blinds and intricate check systems. Instead, I wanted to demonstrate the power that lies at the heart of each of us, something we can all experience right here, right now. I'm no different from anyone else—of this, I'm sure. So if this could happen to me, it could happen to anyone.

And all this led to the book you're holding now. It seems the conversation that started was a powerful and important one, and I'm happy to see that all over the world there's tremendous interest in experiencing Oneness . . . consistently and profoundly.

If you haven't seen the movie yet, it might be a good place to begin. You can visit my Website (**www.jamestwyman.com**) and follow the links, or go to YouTube and search for *"The Proof Movie."* Most of all, I hope you dive into the 40-day program. This, to me, is far more vital than any psychic experiment because it shows what you can accomplish, and how mysterious the world really is.

So open your mind, have fun, and get ready to experience the greatest mystery of all—Oneness.

⌁ A BEGINNING ⌁

Take a deep breath and relax. As you slowly read these words, let your mind loosen and your thoughts recede, and become aware of a feeling deep within you . . . at the center of your chest, a feeling that so often remains hidden, out of sight. Each breath is now directed to this secret and sacred chamber, and you feel it beginning to expand and awaken as if suddenly filled with energy. Like a radiating ball of light, it begins to spread—first into your torso, then your head, now down your arms and legs. And as it moves throughout your body, all the tension that seemed so real a moment ago begins to disappear, dissolving into the wave of light that gently overtakes you. Rest for a moment. Before you read any further, allow this feeling to intensify until you begin to sense that nothing else exists.

And now that you're in this state of perfect peace, it's time to ask yourself a question: *What do I really want out of life?* If you had a nicer car or bigger house, would this feeling you're experiencing right now be more profound? If you lived in a different city and were sitting at this very moment in the most luxurious chair in the world, would you be any more content? Try to resist any thoughts or judgments that may come into your mind, such as: *Well, there's nothing wrong with having a bigger house or more money to buy an extravagant chair.* If anything like that did enter your mind, you may also notice that the ball of light at the center of your chest dimmed a bit. If so, clear your mind and take a couple of deep breaths, relaxing yourself once again. (This is just a short experiment and will be over before you know it. You can return to your thoughts and concerns as soon as it's finished. For now, just relax, and stay with the process.)

What do I really want out of life? This may be the most important question we ask ourselves. We've been trained to seek worldly riches, equating affluence with inner peace. However, it doesn't take long to recall individuals we've met over the years who have achieved profound levels of success and who have secured enormous wealth, but who are among the most unhappy people on Earth. And it doesn't take long to realize that monetary wealth alone won't satisfy us. It doesn't bring us any closer to true happiness or joy.

So if it's not money or success that drives you, what do you truly desire? Take a deep breath, ask this question one more time, and really listen to the answer. What is it that fills your life with the contentment that you're seeking, the love that makes everything worthwhile, and the deep happiness that inspires a sense of satisfaction that transcends the world?

I have the feeling that the answer will be very similar for each and every one of us, regardless of where we dwell or how we choose to live our lives. The words may be different, but they all point in the same direction: *Connection, Harmony, Peace, Oneness.* There is a bond that exists between us, an unseen link that unites and satisfies us in ways nothing else can. In the end, what we're seeking isn't the riches of the world, but the richness of our Souls; and this can only come from realizing that we are connected and whole. Simply put: *we are One.*

Prove it!

Now we're heading in a much more interesting direction. We've heard it all before in a thousand different ways: separation is an illusion; we're really connected, related, whole. It's easy to disprove these ideas as fantasy—the entire world is proof that we are, in fact, unrelated, independent, isolated, and alone. Each of us has a separate body with a unique personality. We live in different cities and countries, and we sometimes fight wars to maintain the separation that we cherish. To say that none of this is real is nothing short of ridiculous, shortsighted, and weak-minded. In other words, it's dead wrong.

So then why have all of the deep thinkers and mystics of the world's great traditions proclaimed the opposite? Why have they spat in the face of conventional thinking and said things like this:

> *"A person experiences life as something separated from the rest—a kind of optical delusion of consciousness. Our task must be to free ourselves from this self-imposed prison, and through compassion, to find the reality of Oneness."*
>
> **— Albert Einstein**

> *"All things share the same breath—the beast, the tree, the man. . . . The air shares its spirit with all the life it supports."*
>
> — attributed to **Chief Seattle**

> *"God is in the innermost part of each and every thing, only in its innermost part, and he alone is One."*
>
> **— Meister Eckhart**

> *"Now are we one with Him Who is our Source."*
>
> — from ***A Course in Miracles***

Is it possible that these wise individuals knew something that we do not? Is there even a remote chance that their eyes were open a little wider than ours, and that they were able to see something that's still invisible to our limited perspectives?

This book is called *The Proof* because I'm going to offer undeniable evidence that the mystics and saints were right: we really are connected and whole. You already know where this experiment began—my attempt to find a book that was secretly hidden in the continental United States, using only my skills of tuning in to the thoughts of the person who hid it. (Reread the Preface if you aren't aware of the film version of *The Proof*.) No words were spoken, and the experiment was completely unrehearsed. It was also something that had never been attempted before, on a scale that made the chances of success seem beyond remote. In the end, it turned out to be an easy task, which I'll explain in more detail as we progress. I found the book hidden in a bush in Seattle, Washington, proving that thoughts *can* be shared. And because that's true, we have more evidence that we're not the separate little individuals we thought we were—in reality, we're more powerful than we can imagine.

But it's still not the definitive proof we're looking for. It may have been an impressive experiment, but finding a hidden book in the Pacific Northwest doesn't change the world. It may be curious—and for some, even a bit scary—but there has to be more; it must be experienced by more than just one person. In fact, it needs to be experienced by *you*, since that's the only way you're going to finally believe.

The real Proof, what you're really searching for, won't come from anything or anyone outside you. You are the Proof that you're seeking.

There's a longing that you've felt from the time you were born, perhaps even before you were born. Every person on Earth has felt that same longing, although it may be incorrectly identified or misunderstood. Is it possible that this is the proof we're all looking for, our Souls' desire for more than what earthly possessions can offer . . . the longing of eternity? Is it possible that it has been within us all along?

This book will help bring you a step closer to finding that place of Oneness within yourself. Ultimately, there isn't anything I can write that will resolutely demonstrate the ways in which your five senses have been misleading you all this time—and that there's another sense, what I call your *Soul sense,* that has the ability to widen the horizon of your consciousness, showing you a vision of the world you've never seen before. Once you experience that new world, you can't go back. Once you learn this lesson, you'll never be able to forget it or deny what you can suddenly so clearly see.

This book is written in two parts and has two very different intentions. The second section is a detailed study of how you can re-create my experiment so that you can experience being connected with others to the point that you're able to read their thoughts (and you can prove this by finding an object they've hidden). There are three levels to this process, and I'm convinced that nearly everyone will experience success with at least one. With a little practice, you'll be able to have a friend hide something in a house, building, or large room; and after a few moments of walking with him or her at your side, you'll discover the item. It's an amazing experience that demonstrates a deep and important lesson, but it's not ultimately true proof of *Oneness.*

That will come from the exercises you'll find in the first section. One of the most essential things that will lead directly to your transformation is *consistency.* In other words, you need to retrain your mind to perceive everything through the lens of the Soul rather than the ego. Your ego is the part of you that sees everything as separate—alone and in competition with you. Your Soul knows that nothing is truly separate; and that on the deepest, most essential level, we are One. Unfortunately, however, you've been trained to give the ego's vision much more power than the Soul's, and so the evidence that surrounds you is overlooked and ignored.

But what would happen if you retrained yourself to see the world like the saints and mystics? How would things appear? How would your life change? The goal of Part I is to provide you with 40 days of consistent restructuring, teaching you to see everything in a new—or perhaps a very ancient—way.

I believe that it's the most natural thing in the universe, and that we were taught from a very early age to deny the Soul's vision of the world and focus instead on the symbols of separation.

When we were born and for the first period of our lives, we had no concept of separation. Everything we perceived was an extension of who we are rather than a distant and alien body we can neither realize nor understand. It's time to reverse this momentum and remember our original innocence—the sight and vision we beheld when we were born, which is still within us.

"Where two or more are gathered . . ."

Part I of this book ("The 40-Day Oneness Program") is written in a dialogue format. I believe that it's often through joining with the Soul of another that the most essential wisdom can be discovered. That's why I asked Anakha Coman—teacher, mystic, and friend—to join me in this endeavor. I've known Anakha for many years, and I trust her unique and profound connection with the eternal. She is a minister who lives in Portland, Oregon; and she was the first person who came to mind when I considered who might offer the highest, clearest demonstration of Oneness. Together she and I broke down this process of discovering Oneness into 40 aspects, carefully exploring their intricate qualities through a conversation that took place over several days. Anakha then designed a set of 40 daily practices and "I AM" affirmations to enable you to fully experience and embody Oneness at the heart of your very own life.

Through exercises, discussion, and your own commitment to transform your mind, these 40 practices will give you the momentum you need to enter into the stream of Oneness that is all around you but which is often missed.

How to Best Experience This Book

As you already know, this book is divided into two distinct sections. The first contains the 40-day course on experiencing Oneness. If you dedicate yourself to this process, you'll discover an entirely new existence where separation loses its allure and

Oneness is the guiding principle. Simply put, you'll experience what the saints and sages from antiquity have described as *enlightenment.*

Does that sound too grandiose? You probably didn't expect such claims when you picked up this book. You may have simply wished to learn how to read another person's mind, as if that was the pinnacle of what you could achieve. It's only the first step, and the more you realize this, the faster you'll be able to ascend to the higher lessons where you can experience a sense of Oneness that you never dreamed existed. This is Anakha's and my intent and genuine focus of the 40-day program.

But I also won't neglect the goal of finding an object that has been hidden by another person. To me, this allows you to experience the process, to help you gauge your progress through the course. Therefore, I recommend that you read this book in a slightly different manner. Begin by engaging in several of the initial practices, initiating the 40-day process. At some point, perhaps after several days, you'll feel the energy begin to build and your confidence increase. That will be the sign that it's time to engage the second part of the program—reading another person's mind, obtaining the tangible proof that you aren't separate as you may have believed, but that you can actually share thoughts and impressions with another Soul. Continue to read and experience the lessons as you go through the exercises. The two parts work together in dissolving the barriers between your ego and your Soul, revealing a deep sense of Oneness that will change your life forever.

I AM Statements

Throughout the 40-day practice period, you'll have the opportunity to engage in "I AM" statements, which are meant to take the lessons deeper. In 2008 I wrote a book called *The Moses Code* that examined the inherent power of the phrase *I AM* in detail. These simple words are from one of the first recorded conversations with

God that took place more than 3,500 years ago. When God tasked Moses with delivering the Israelites from slavery, Moses realized that he needed proof; he needed to convince the Pharaoh and his own people that this was indeed the will of God. So for the first time, he asked God for his name, and God replied, *"Ehyeh Asher Ehyeh,"* which is often translated to: "I AM THAT, I AM."

You'll notice that contrary to its common form, I've placed a comma in the middle, emphasizing the two phrases: *I AM THAT* and *I AM*. I've demonstrated how the use of I AM statements has a profound effect in attracting energy into your life, manifesting whatever you focus upon. When combined with the ancient name of God, the power is staggering.

If you'd like more information on harnessing this Divine energy, I suggest you read my book *The Moses Code*. For now, it's only important that you know that claiming anything you desire by saying "I AM that," as opposed to "I want that" or "I hope I can have that someday" is one of the most spiritually potent tools you can discover. Each practice in Part I will end with at least one "I AM" statement that will help you fully comprehend the lesson and integrate it into your life.

Open your eyes now!

It may be hard to believe that a book can provide a 40-day program for embodying Oneness and enlightenment. I've always believed that what seems impossible to the ego has already been accomplished by the Soul, and it may be wise to employ this philosophy at the onset of this journey. You are already One with everything you perceive—with the people you see as you walk down the street; with every situation you encounter; and with the Source of all Creation, sometimes known as God. If you're able to lay aside your critical mind—even for a short while—you may discover something that you always suspected but were afraid to truly entertain: *Oneness*. It's right there within you, and now it's time to open the door so that it can finally be released into the world.

⌒ PART I ⌒

THE 40-DAY ONENESS PROGRAM

James: It's time to enter into a process of deep transformation. I suggested earlier that you begin with at least a few of these lessons before learning how to read another person's thoughts for a very good reason: it's important to understand why you're trying to do it in the first place. Hopefully, it's not to impress someone else, because if it is, it probably won't work as well as you might think. If your goal is to use these experiments to understand and experience Oneness, then you're on the right track. That's the purpose of these 40 lessons—to give you a tangible experience of Oneness, then help you incorporate it into your everyday life. At that point, it will make very little difference if you're able to find a book, or anything else that might be hidden by another person. You will have integrated the real lesson—that you aren't separate from any other person . . . or even God. If this is the goal you seek, then you've come to the right place.

The question immediately rises to the surface: What is Oneness? Is it an ethereal state that's more imaginary than concrete? Is it something we can write or read about but not actually realize or attain? Or is it something much more immediate, like an object that was hidden directly in front of us, so obviously placed that we miss it altogether? The fact is that we've been hiding from Oneness from the very beginning, afraid of what we may have to give up if we finally decide to dive into this boundless ocean. In the end, nothing needs to be sacrificed except the willingness to live small; and this is where we begin, with small steps and simple exercises that help us sense the gentle approach of this precious state.

So, Anakha, how would you describe the Soul's longing for Oneness, as well as our seeming obsession with avoiding it by being weak and separate?

Anakha: The way I'm experiencing it in this moment is as a longing of the heart, a longing to remember. Oneness is a process of remembering the natural state we experienced before we were born or when we were in the womb—a time when we were fully living that innate, natural connection. It's also a time when we trusted that connection to meet our needs—a time when we felt safe and secure. I think part of what contributes to our sense of disconnection is the natural separation we experienced when we were born, and for the first time, having to struggle for our caregiver's attention to get our needs met. That sets up a natural separation, which also produces fear within many people.

In addition to being a longing of the heart, Oneness is a *condition* of the heart, a willingness to open up to both the blessings and the challenges of Oneness. This requires that we reclaim an inherent faith in ourselves, in life, and in each other . . . trusting that Oneness will support, love, and nourish us. This is our connection to one another. This also opens us to the vulnerability of Oneness. For when we open our hearts and minds to the sense of interconnectedness, we experience both the beauty of Oneness *and* the challenge of Oneness. We allow ourselves to experience heartbreak because when we actually feel the condition of our collective humanity, we connect to the violence, abuse, and neglect that many people are experiencing around the world *and* in our own backyards.

James: You speak of the longing we feel, and I think this is something that everyone can relate to. Each one of us, from the time we are born, or at least as long as we can remember, has felt this longing. It's something that we sense deep within, but we usually dissociate and become attached to the things that lie outside of us instead of what lies within. And we think that maybe we can fill that longing with goods rather than realizing the *goodness* within. This is what brings us closer to Oneness.

If there's proof that Oneness is real, I would say that this longing we feel is it. We somehow know this already, and it's that desire for what we cannot realize on the outside that shows us that we are indeed connected to something within.

Anakha: As you're speaking, James, I'm thinking of a kind of nostalgia for the unity that we know lives within us—and, yes, that we've often been seeking outside ourselves. This is about receptivity to the truth because Oneness just *is*. Oneness is an *isness*. It isn't something that we have to struggle with or strive for; it requires a softening, a slowing, a relaxing, and an opening into that reality.

Yet so often we've become acclimated to a very fast pace (especially in Western culture), moving outside what I call the *rhythm of the heart*. We're not actually moving in a state of Oneness—that is, we're not in the place and pace where we feel and connect to our natural way of living.

The practices and exercises we're going to introduce will help bring that awareness and remembrance back into the body, mind, and heart. These are simple practices that can be easily applied and used every day. We don't have to go to the monastery for 40 days and nights or spend two hours a day meditating—although those may be useful and powerful experiences. The following Oneness practices are designed to be integrated and applied in our normal day-to-day lives—what I call *microspiritual practices*. We can truly make the heart of Oneness, this spiritual truth, a living reality in the midst of our lives, including when we're working, playing with our children, shopping, driving, and doing any of the other things that fill our busy days. Practicing the presence of Oneness becomes a moment-to-moment, spontaneous prayer and conversation with God and with all Life.

James: You mentioned going into a monastery for 40 days. There are so many stories of the mystics and saints, and even Jesus, going into the desert for 40 days or 40 years . . . that particular number shows up time and again throughout history. It represents transformation. And so what we're going to offer here are 40 practices to soften our attachment to separation so that we can realize the inherent Oneness that is our foundation, our life, the Source of our being. As you mentioned, Anakha, these are simple exercises we can incorporate into our lives right now. That being said, let's begin by taking a closer look at the first 20 practices.

The First 20 Practices:
A Place to Begin

These first 20 lessons are focused on generating a field of Oneness and applying these practices in the moment-to-moment aspects and experiences of our lives. Through these practices, we create a metaphysical bank account and begin making deposits into the "Bank of Oneness." We're actually manifesting a "field of grace" that's moving and sustaining us; as well as working in, through, and as us the more we commit ourselves to these practices.

Once we consciously activate the field of Oneness, just like in nature, all opposites will show up. When we bring our attention to this consciousness, we'll also begin to see in ourselves and in our relationships all the areas where we're still trapped in separation or constriction—where we're not able to feel that deep connection to the One, to our essential self, and to our brothers and sisters. And as we generate this field, we become sustained in it and develop the courage and confidence to bring this consciousness into the heart of the darkness (or constriction) where fear maintains its grip on us.

The beauty of doing these first 20 practices before we go into the darker places is that we find ourselves buoyed and lifted by the consciousness of Oneness itself. We aren't required to do the work of looking at this on our own; we don't have to engage in that heavy lifting. It's really a gentle observation of where we are still in fear and how we're extending it to our everyday experiences and in relating with others. Through that observation, we can start to feel the flow of Oneness and bring the energies of love to that place of unlove—that darkness and constriction.

These first 20 lessons are a gentle step into the heart of Oneness. Once there, you'll find that you're beginning to open in profound new ways, and you'll feel the energy of life embrace you in a manner that defies reason. You don't need to understand this with your logical mind—you only need to embrace it with your whole self. Once you do so, you'll feel the transformation occur on its own, without your conscious effort. In other words, Oneness itself will grab on to you and pull you into a new world, a place that you never left except in your imagination.

Open your eyes now—perhaps for the very first time—and embrace these practices like you would a dear friend. Your life is about to change forever.

THE RHYTHM
OF ONENESS

*"Happiness is not a matter of intensity, but
of balance and order and rhythm and harmony."*

— **Thomas Merton**

"Smile, breathe, and go slowly."

— **Thich Nhat Hanh**

*"Even in the middle of a hurricane, the bottom of the
sea is calm. As the storm rages and the winds howl, the
deep waters sway in gentle rhythm, a light movement
of fish and plant life. Below there is no storm."*

— **Wayne Muller**

James: There is a natural rhythm to life that gives us a tangible experience of Oneness. We felt it when we were born and when we were young, but as we grew, we realized that the evidence around us painted a very different picture. This evidence led us to believe that we're in competition with every person and situation we encounter. This is how the ego was born, and we nurtured it because we thought we needed its protection. But in reality we were simply out of rhythm, and Oneness felt like a distant dream. Now that we realize this, we can enter back into the stream and sense that natural rhythm again.

So, Anakha, earlier you were speaking about the Oneness we felt when we were born and when we were small . . . and that we had to actually learn separation. I'd like us to talk about that a bit more. This was a natural condition—something we needed while we were young, wasn't it?

Anakha: Yes. When we watch children, we see that they are certainly in, and are accepting of, their own rhythm. They're deeply in touch with their basic needs, whether it's for food, attention, comfort, or rest. They're also wide open to the flow of their emotions. One minute they may be sad, the next minute mad, and the next, joyfully laughing and playing. Children allow themselves to move at their natural rhythm and pace. They accept what arrives from moment to moment and then allow it to spontaneously flow into something else.

It's quite a beautiful experience to observe children in that place of Oneness. Yet what happens when we're young is that we start to interact with the world, our parents, and our primary caregivers; and in that process, our experiences tell us that we're less than whole . . . that something is wrong with us, we're not enough, or we're not doing "it" right. And from those events a core belief of fear is created. We start mistrusting our inner rhythm, our essence, our natural state, our emotions, our truth . . . and we begin trying to fit into something that will guarantee our safety, security, acceptance, and well-being.

The journey into Oneness includes identifying and dissolving those limiting beliefs that were created early on. Most often they aren't even in our conscious awareness. They live just below our awareness in the subconscious; and they have a powerful impact on how we show up in the world, and how we act and relate to others. When we begin slowing our rhythm and discovering our natural pace—our automatic way of moving, speaking, and breathing—we reconnect to the state of Oneness.

James: One of the things I'm feeling right now is the importance of not judging these natural rhythms. We must know that they're natural and vital to the evolution of our Souls. Allow the state of remembering and forgetting. We came here to forget who we are for a moment so that in remembering Oneness we may appreciate it more deeply.

I think this is really the journey of the Soul. So we don't want to look at the way that we've lived—our ego existence—as wrong or bad because that actually makes it difficult to release or transform it. I think we have to accept and love ourselves exactly as we are. At that point, we're ready to remember, ready to step out of that state of forgetfulness and think back to why we were born, why we're here. And then we can activate that knowledge in our lives and in the world.

Anakha: Beautiful . . . yes! It's a process. The rhythm of Oneness will bring us back into love and tenderness for ourselves and one another. And yes, there's already enough pain surrounding how we've lived within the illusion of separation—we certainly don't need to add insult to injury. Compassion is absolutely necessary as we allow those beliefs that have manifested as separation in our lives to actually begin to heal and dissolve.

Exercise

Returning to your natural rhythm and moving with the pace of the universal heartbeat restores you to Oneness. Slowing down connects you with the rhythm of Life, with your essential self, and with other people. Holding yourself in this way brings you into the very heart of Oneness.

There's a close connection between the rhythm of Oneness and the rhythm of your footsteps, your breathing, and your mind. Today, practice finding a pace that connects you with your breath, heart, and mind . . . truly connecting with your natural rhythm and flow. Notice when you feel your movements becoming forced and harried. Within that gentle awareness, take a moment to pause and return to your center. Breathe and rest for a moment in the stillness. Repeat the word *ahimsa* (meaning nonviolent actions) as a mantra throughout your day as you continue to return again and again to the rhythm of Oneness.

Imagine this practice as a moving meditation, like tai chi, or as a flowing dance, such as ballet. Allow one action to create and flow effortlessly into the next. Every breath, step, and thought is connected. As you engage in this practice, the frenetic pace of your thoughts will become slower and calm down; and your breathing will become fuller and more relaxed. You'll experience the beauty, vitality, and energy of life. You'll feel connected to your own deep personal integrity and to the integrity of life that surrounds you. In this place, you're moving within ahimsa—expressing compassion to yourself and others—and you're in union with all things. Paradoxically, when you slow your pace to your natural rhythm, your movements become more graceful, powerful, and focused— thus, more is accomplished, created, and received with less effort and energy.

For today, experiment with pace, rhythm, and movement. Discover the rhythm of Oneness for yourself and share it with others.

Affirmation

I AM moving with the rhythm of my heart, in harmony with the purpose of my Soul, vibrating with all of creation.

⤙ PRACTICE 2 ⤚

THE BREATH
OF ONENESS

*"All the principles of heaven and earth are living
inside you. Life itself is truth, and this will never
change. Everything in heaven and earth breathes.
Breath is the thread that ties creation together."*

— Morihei Ueshiba

*"Ancient lovers believed a kiss would literally unite their souls,
because the spirit was said to be carried in one's breath."*

— Eve Glicksman

*"Breath is the bridge which connects life to
consciousness, which unites your body to your thoughts."*

— Thich Nhat Hanh

James: Following one's breath is one of the primary focuses of almost any meditation practice. It's also a wonderful way to understand Oneness. We breathe in and out, and although these are separate actions, we need to do both to survive. If our breath went in one direction only, we'd die. Yet they are really the same. If we follow the breath and use it as our focus throughout the day, it can help us stay in a state of active relaxation; thus, we can sense Oneness to a greater degree.

Anakha: The breath of Oneness connects us in all directions. It connects us in the present moment to ourselves, to those who have come before us, to those who are here with us now, and even to those who will come after us. It's a beautiful process: connecting internally and vertically by breathing in the Spirit of God; and also experiencing a horizontal, external link to each other through our breath. We are united through the simple awareness that we're all actually breathing in life together.

For all the differences we might experience on the planet today, there are basic experiences we share. Everyone, in this very moment, is breathing in life. That's really beautiful when I think about that . . . about really connecting in that sameness, in that Oneness, to my brothers and sisters around the world.

James: I like your explanation of "breathing in life together." When you think about it, every time we breathe we're taking in at least a million atoms that were also breathed in by Jesus, the Buddha, Gandhi, and every other person who has ever lived. Every single breath connects us with every other person and every other being who has ever lived on this planet. So each breath we take literally links us to a state of Oneness, not just in theory, but in actual physical practice. So we can use our breath throughout the normal course of our day to remember Oneness . . . just by being aware as we breathe, acknowledging our connection with every person who lives now or has ever lived.

Anakha: That's beautiful. If I'm consciously breathing with and even for different people or places around the planet—I'm thinking of Israel, for example—then through this awareness, through my love-filled breath, I can begin circulating my compassion to Israel or to any of the areas on the planet that are experiencing separation, conflict, or war.

What if I'm able to circulate love just through my conscious breathing? You'll notice, when you start to breathe with another, that you can actually change and regulate the pace and depth of the other person's breathing. As I was practicing this morning, I started to become aware of different places on the planet. I could actually feel my heart soften as I experienced genuine compassion being born out of Oneness through conscious contact with my very own breath.

James: So the breath of Oneness is a tangible way we can begin the softening of our own hearts in order to feel this state of Oneness that's all around us . . . something we can apply to the most ordinary moments of our lives.

Exercise

Begin this practice by becoming aware of your breath, expanding it throughout your entire body. Allow your breathing to organically circulate, connecting cells and organs, blood and bones. Feel the beauty and elegance of your body's intricate design. Through each inhale and exhale, allow yourself to be filled by the Spirit and filled with Oneness . . . then permit yourself to become empty, in Spirit and in Oneness.

The Hebrew word for breath is *ruach,* but it also signifies spirit and wind. It is your breath that connects you with Spirit and your Soul. It sustains your Soul. Now, with your breath, animate and give expression to your Soul, knowing that breath and Soul are from one origin. Allow yourself to be filled with the breath of Oneness, which is love, joy, peace, and unity. Exhale separation; inhale Oneness. Exhale fear and anxiety; inhale God's loving presence and power.

Imagine that you're breathing with every living being and organism on the planet and in the cosmos. Breathe with the trees and with the ocean. Breathe with the children in Africa. Breathe with the monks in Tibet. Breathe with the saints and mystics from the past: Jesus, Buddha, Krishna, Moses, and Muhammad. Breathe with your friends, family, and community. Breathe with those you consider "different." Breathe with the planets and stars. Breathe with all of creation and know the truth of *I AM One. We are One.* Come alive with the breath of Oneness! Dedicate your breathing as a prayer for all sentient beings. Allow a single word or phrase to arise on your lips, and send it out to the world through the breath of Oneness. In this practice, your breathing becomes a prayer and a profound act of sacred activism.

Practice the breath of Oneness for at least five minutes at the beginning and end of your day and your Soul will settle into a heavenly peace. Return to it often throughout the day in order to practice the presence of God wherever you are and in whatever you're doing.

Affirmations

I AM breathing Life, and Life is breathing me.

I AM forever connected to my Soul
in the Spirit of Life. I AM, I AM, I AM.

⌒ PRACTICE 3 ⌒

THE SOUND
OF ONENESS

*"Every element has a sound, an original
sound from the order of God; all those sounds
unite like the harmony from harps and zithers."*

— **Hildegard of Bingen**

*"We need to find God, and he cannot be found
in noise and restlessness. God is the friend of silence.
See how nature—trees, flowers, grass—grows in silence;
see the stars, the moon, and the sun, how they move in
silence. . . . We need silence to be able to touch souls."*

— **Mother Teresa**

"The first stage of worship is silence."

— **Muhammad**

James: The last thing our ego wants is that we be still or quiet. It much prefers that we stay preoccupied with the busyness of life. Our Soul, on the other hand, listens deeply and thrives on silence. Everything blends together, and we begin to remember our most natural state—the one we experienced when we were born, when we felt Oneness with amazing clarity and ease. If we spent even a few minutes a day being still, listening intently to our heart, our breath, or whatever is around us, we'd begin to hear the sound of Oneness once again.

So I think at this stage, a short discussion on the differences between the ego and the Soul would probably serve us well in order to understand what it is we're releasing as well as what we're bringing into our lives.

Anakha, how would you describe the ego?

Anakha: Well, I'll describe the ego in the way in which I experience it. For myself, I feel it when I'm in a constricted place, disconnected from the truth that "I am love" and "I am whole and complete." The ego is a place where I encounter the fear that I'm not good enough, I'm not supported in life, I don't belong, and that I don't know how to connect with others. All of those wounded places—those fearful ways of thinking—that constrict my breath and heart and shift my rhythm into something unnatural . . . those are the moments when I'm in ego.

Ego tells me that who I AM isn't enough and never will be. At some level, I think we all share that same core fear: that we aren't good enough, smart enough, beautiful enough, talented enough . . . whatever it might be. The ego speaks through the voice of lack, limitation, and "not enoughness." However, the Soul (when we're truly grounded and connected) whispers the most beautiful consolations and affirmations of our wholeness, completeness, and of our belonging. The Soul tells us that who we are in this moment is absolutely who we were born to be.

James: Most of us have heard this acronym for the ego: Edging God Out. And if we think of God as that perfect state of Oneness, then the ego is edging Oneness out, for it creates the need to remain separate. It's ironic that the constriction and fear of the ego—in trying to protect itself—actually maintains that isolation. If we could just relax into our Soul and hold still for a moment, then the unfolding into Oneness becomes easy and natural. It's not something we need to *do;* it's something we need to *be.* The ego constricts, whereas the Soul expands. And that expansion is the most natural thing we could ever accomplish.

Anakha: I'm reminded of Andrew Harvey's term "Coca-Coma," which refers to all the numbing distractions and busyness of our everyday lives, and how our drive to consume is an attempt to avoid the core fears of the ego and the powerful messages of the Soul. That's what motivates us to push ourselves to acquire, achieve, and compete in order to compensate for fears and wounds.

It's truly a powerful form of sacred activism and spiritual peacemaking to find times throughout the day—even if it's just a couple of minutes—to unplug from the hysteria of the collective ego and the manifestation of fear in the world; and return to a true knowing of Oneness, wholeness, and wellness. It's so easy to get caught up in whatever the drama of the day might be and start to move outside of the rhythm and breath of Oneness. That's why coming into that stillness—that silence—and deepening into our hearts is where we'll actually hear the sound of Oneness—our Soul—speak to us.

Exercise

The journey into the internal temple of your heart—your innermost being—begins and ends in silence. With this practice, seek the solitude within and find refuge in the arms of God—the contemplative embrace of Oneness. In the silence, you touch the still point and lie in the green pastures of your Soul. Within this sacred place, hear the sound of Oneness. These are the whispers from Spirit . . . whispers of truth and faith that reassure you that all is One and all is well.

Today's practice can be applied in a quiet setting in nature, in a taxicab, or during a business meeting. Practicing inner stillness in the midst of your day infuses the consciousness of Oneness into the core of your life. This practice brings the power and presence of God into each situation you encounter and into all areas of your life: health, relationships, career, and finances. Silent retreats and Sabbath practices are also rich experiences that can expand your ability to connect with Oneness.

Begin this practice by slowing your pace, deepening your breath, and opening your awareness to the present moment. Allow your thoughts to calm and drift through your mind in slow motion. Follow the spiral movement of your breath inward into the interior castle of your heart. Your heart is always listening; it's a universal resource of deep communication. Continue to breathe yourself into inner silence and stillness, seeking and unlocking your Soul. Feel your own inner terrain, the landscape of life within you. Breathe. Inhale and exhale. Let go and let the silence take you now, pulling you deeper and deeper into your inner sanctuary. Seek it as it seeks you. Be still. Rest in the I AM as you silently breathe, listening to the sound of Oneness.

Trust what arises . . . have faith in your inner hearing. Be receptive to the whispers, the voice of inspired guidance, the consolations from the angels, and the truth of your own essential voice. Pay attention and receive. Allow the sound of Oneness to rejuvenate, restore, and repattern your heart, Soul, and mind. Breathe. Be still and know I AM.

From this inner sanctuary of silence, allow any questions you have for the Divine to slowly rise, simply and effortlessly. Guidance is as near as your own breath. Listen. Receive. Believe. *Who am I? Why am I here? What is calling to me? Who must I now become in consciousness?*

Allow your own sound of Oneness to be expressed, and feel its vibration deep in your heart. Give voice to it; know that it is your song to learn, to sing, and to share.

Return again and again throughout the day to your inner sanctuary of silence. This place is always within you and is one of your most precious resources. Use this practice to cultivate the Presence, and you'll discover that Oneness speaks in silence.

Affirmation

I AM the sound of silence, listening to the sweet whispers of my Soul telling me that all is One, all is well, and I AM loved.

THE GAZE OF ONENESS

"With enraptured gaze we beheld the white moon rising quietly behind the tall trees, the silvery rays it was casting upon sleeping nature, the bright stars twinkling in the deep skies, the light breath of the evening breeze making the snowy clouds float easily along; all this raised our souls to heaven."

— St. Thérèse of Lisieux

"When the eyes of the heart are opened, the creation is revealed as it really is . . . the body of Divine Light."

— Andrew Harvey

"The day of my spiritual awakening was the day I saw and knew I saw all things in God and God in all things."

— Mechthild of Magdeburg

James: Have you ever openly and honestly gazed into another person's eyes without any judgment at all? If you look long enough, you might begin to feel a deep sense of connection or compassion with that person, even a feeling of Oneness. What if you stared into your own eyes in the same way? Perhaps if you gazed into the mirror, you would allow yourself to see the depths of your own heart and Soul.

If everyone could practice this in their daily lives—seeing the Divine within each other—even for brief moments, how would our lives change? How would that affect the world?

Anakha: I think there's such a hunger to be seen, heard, and received . . . a hunger for true presence. In these times of constant activity, challenge, and stress (even with the things we enjoy), just to have someone who's present and still with us—seeing and perceiving us for who we really are—is such a rare and amazing gift. One of our most powerful possessions in the "medicine bag" of Oneness is our ability to be present . . . to see and receive another individual in his or her essential nature without judgment or expectation. To be in that place of *Namaste* (seeing Christ in each other) begins by viewing ourselves through that very lens. It makes it extremely hard to receive another person as an expression of Oneness, an expression of the Divine, if we aren't able to also perceive it in ourselves.

James: I think this idea of being present is so critically important to accepting and experiencing Oneness in our lives. There's nothing more seductive and compelling than someone who's fully in the moment. If we're with a lover who's completely in the now, it's one of the most exciting and beautiful gifts we can receive. And, of course, because giving and receiving are essentially the same thing, when we allow ourselves to be the access point for another, we're also serving as the access point for ourselves.

I'm able to gaze upon another being and see myself as I really am. I think that's the significance of the gaze of Oneness: the ability to see yourself through another, using every moment as an opportunity for accessing Oneness in your life.

Anakha: That's lovely. I'm thinking about how everyone in our lives is a teacher on the path of Oneness. I don't just mean the lessons we glean through our everyday interactions, but that we're also watching each other in order to learn how to make our way in the world. Consciously, and often unconsciously, we're teaching. When we lift our awareness and remember to be rooted in Oneness, we offer an invitation to others to actually access their own Oneness.

By embracing this, we're demonstrating a new way of being. We can start a grassroots "Revolution in Oneness" and allow it to ripple out so that it includes more and more people! I do believe that through our presence we provide a vital access point for others to experience Oneness.

Exercise

French philosopher Pierre Teilhard de Chardin said: "Nothing here below is profane for those who know how to see." Do *you* know how to see? Are you willing to look upon yourself and your life with the gaze of Oneness? Are you willing to remove the scales of separation from your eyes and recognize the Divine within?

For today you are invited—*urged*—to see yourself and all the conditions of your life (those that you may judge as good *and* bad) through the enraptured and awakened gaze of Oneness. View everything as connected and divinely ordered, conspiring on your behalf to bring you into alignment with your truest self and highest good. Imagine that nothing within you or your life is outside of Oneness; therefore, perceive all things as sacred and holy. Give thanks for this sweet perfection.

To increase your awareness, consciously observe the expressions of beauty and creativity that surround you. Gaze with awe into a starry nighttime sky. Notice the fragile courage of the first crocus of spring. Wonder at the symmetry of a snowflake or the complexity of a newborn. From head to toe, look upon your own body with adoration. Seek the beauty that lies within a billboard, a streetcar, a puppy, a doughnut shop, a blade of grass; for each of these holds the aura of the sacred. Know the truth: this physical, palpable world is indeed a Divine place. You are standing on holy ground. Affirm that all things on Earth are part of God's holy creation.

Look upon everything with the all-adoring, awakened, and curious gaze of Oneness. Learning to see in this way is central to an understanding of God's love for the world and the life it sustains. Today, awaken the gaze of Oneness within you. Soften your eyes and perceive with your heart. Behold Christ and receive all with Namaste. Rejoice in your transformed sight!

Affirmation

I AM perceiving the world with an awakened and enraptured gaze.
I see myself in God and I see God in all things. Namaste.

THE HEART OF ONENESS

"Love is the essence of all creeds; the true mystic welcomes it whatever guise it may assume. . . . I follow the religion of Love, whichever way his camels take."

— **Ibn al-'Arabī**

"Love is the affinity which links and draws together the elements of the world. . . . Love, in fact, is the agent of universal synthesis."

— **Pierre Teilhard de Chardin**

"Love is the offspring of spiritual affinity and unless that affinity is created in a moment, it will not be created in years or even generations."

— **Kahlil Gibran**

James: What would happen if you spent an hour a day walking around your city or neighborhood, or wherever you find yourself, viewing everyone through the lens of Oneness? How about a half hour? Even a few minutes would be enough to open your heart and help you perceive the deeper impulses that the ego can't understand, but of which the heart is fully aware. And once your heart is open, how would that change the way you live or interact with others?

We spend so much of our time reserved and shut down that we forget that openness is the most natural and wondrous way of living. When our hearts are open, we automatically see what we'd normally miss—the Oneness that is always present.

When people ask, "What's a simple meditation I can practice every day that will change my life?" this is how I usually respond: "Spend a few minutes a day just walking around, seeing the beloved (or Christ or God) in everyone you meet." The beautiful thing is that at first this appears to be a metaphor, but it's not one at all—it's reality. It's real, and we can feel it deep within us. We sense this immediate link with the other person, and this is one of the most tangible experiences of Oneness.

Anakha: These practices will become a living reality; they're no longer just words on a page or rituals we're enacting. They'll usher us into the heart of Oneness, teaching us a new way of living and being. Changing our perspective from the head to the heart is the journey into Oneness. Our minds are designed to constantly evaluate, judge, separate, and construct. But the heart holds a different intelligence—the wisdom of Oneness. And this is our most powerful tool today.

When we look at the dire conditions of the world, they're actually a reflection of the heart, challenges that come from places where there's an insufficient flow of love. We might have different ways of looking at these difficulties, but when it comes down to it, they're all calls for loving-kindness. It's only through an awakened, illuminated, supple heart that the intelligence of love flows freely. Our hearts know how we can live in Oneness and how it should be expressed in the world. For our economy, educational system, international relations . . . there are inspiring ideas and solutions that can only be perceived and received through an awakened heart.

James: I like how you describe this as a living reality flowing into the ordinary world. And I think of how it can transform our world—our political and social systems, and of course, our families. I think that living in a state of Oneness is another way of saying that we're living in balance. It's important to understand that this is a *dynamic* balance. We sometimes think of being stable or at peace as a static state, something that's even a bit boring. Who wants to be in one place all the time . . . it doesn't seem like anything happens! This is why understanding it as a dynamic balance is key. It doesn't mean that it's stationary; rather, it moves back and forth. A dynamic flow exists between us, and this is what makes it a living reality. Our willingness to live it—not just theorize about it—is what creates the access point that moves us into the deeper aspects of Oneness.

Anakha: When you say *access point,* it reminds me that even in the places where we might perceive fear, darkness, and constriction, there is a seed of Oneness. And with an open heart, a receptive heart, we can actually perceive that access point; and from within the separation and through our loving intention, we allow Oneness to be born.

Exercise

Today our hearts stir, knowing that they're the true seat of Oneness. For it's only with an awakened, illuminated, and revealed heart that we can embody Oneness and have the courage to fully penetrate the darkness of separation in ourselves and the world.

Begin by engaging the breath of Oneness, allowing your heart to become open, soft, and supple as the barriers surrounding it dissolve. Your heart is your most precious asset and most power-ful intelligence—a Divine instrument of love and an expression of peace.

Today's practice focuses on breaking down the armor around your heart. In Matthew 7:7, Jesus says: "Ask, and it shall be given you; seek, and you shall find; knock, and it shall be opened unto you." Knock on the door of your heart and allow it to fully open!

Gently bring your attention to your breath. Allow your breath to caress your heart, massaging it with the breath of Oneness. In Aramaic, "Knock and be opened" translates as *Qush Wa Ephphetha* ("koosh wa ef-fa-tah"). *Qush,* "knock," creates the space for the opening of your heart with your sincere intensity. *Ephphetha,* "be opened," emphasizes the process of nature that happens easily and effortlessly.

Knock on the door of your heart, and allow yourself to be opened. Let this be your mantra as you surrender to the process of disarming and dissolving the barriers to your heart.

Begin breathing and chanting: *Qush Wa Ephphetha. Knock and be opened.* Find your pace, your rhythm. Listen and feel your heart center as you as chant these sacred words of devotion. Use either the Aramaic or English translation, or both, depending on what feels right for you:

Qush Wa Ephphetha. Knock and be opened.
Qush Wa Ephphetha. Knock and be opened.
Qush Wa Ephphetha. Knock and be opened.

Continue chanting, breathing, knocking, and opening; feel the resonance deep within and know that your heart is opening. Feel the dam breaking, as love bursts forth to the places where your heart has been walled up in fear. Feel the power and the presence of love grow within you. Observe as your fears and limiting beliefs crumble and are carried away. Love is flowing, infiltrating your old hiding places so that you can finally experience true love.

Let yourself be opened fully! Recite this prayer and withhold nothing; fully and completely surrender into the arms of God, the mystery of Life, the fires of sacred love that burn within you.

Dear God,
I am knocking from the inside,
my heart is opening from the inside.
I wish to be made new.
Resurrected in my wholeness.
Holy Spirit, Maranatha (our Lord cometh).
Come, do your sacred work within me,
within my life,
within my relationships now.
I ask for your grace and for your delicacy as you
breathe new life into my heart.
Qush Wa Ephphetha. Knock and be opened.
Amen.

Affirmation

I AM knocking on the door of my heart, opening to the unimaginable presence and power of Divine Love that lives within me.

THE BODY OF ONENESS

*"Begin to see yourself as a soul with
a body rather than a body with a soul."*

— Dr. Wayne W. Dyer

*"Our bodies know they belong; it is
our minds that make our lives so homeless."*

— John O'Donohue

"The body is a sacred garment."

— Martha Graham

James: We usually think of our bodies as the ultimate symbols of our separation from everything else we perceive. After all, my body looks different from yours. Even if I had a twin, and the average person couldn't tell my sibling and me apart, my mother would always be able to pick up the subtle differences between us.

Although our physical forms do set us apart, there are ways in which our bodies can also help us remember our Oneness, such as when we're in love or when we're making love. What if as I feel my arm or leg, I remember that it's still part of *one* body? Our bodies are like anything else—we can use them to live separately or as One. It's really up to us.

Anakha: For many people, our physical differences illustrate our separateness. Many of us also harbor judgments about, or fears of, our bodies, but a powerful "microcosmic" way to begin connecting with Oneness is to connect with ourselves. As we start to feel in harmony with our bodies, we move into a place of love and acceptance for the beautiful expression of Oneness that our physical forms actually are. We see that each of our parts has a beautiful function and purpose.

We begin to view our bodies as amazing vessels that carry us through the world and offer the most amazing experiences, like watching a sunset, eating a mango, dancing with children, or walking barefoot on a sandy beach. And I think that as our appreciation of the mystery grows, we can take that idea as a metaphor for how the whole world is actually an expression of one body and is working together in that same sort of elegance, precision, and harmony.

Exercise

Your body is an expression of the living Oneness, a temple for the Divine presence. When you're disconnected from yourself, you're out of touch with your essence and nature; and you're not resonating with the rest of the world. This disconnect keeps you from enjoying the many blessings and bliss of Oneness.

Today, take a moment to be still, becoming aware of your breath. Imagine that your body is like a stringed instrument that needs tuning. This adjustment will bring you into presence, putting you back in sync with the world. Being fully present in yourself means being perpetually in tune, ready to vibrate with each moment as it unfolds. Neither rejecting nor preferring any sensation, emotion, or experience, you embrace the Oneness of life. This practice reconnects you to your natural state of wholeness.

Begin by tuning in to your body. Pay attention to any sensations that may appear as tension, energy, deadness, numbness, aliveness, pleasure, or any other emotion. Allow yourself to become present to your body, gently noticing your judgments, fears, distractions, and projections as they float to the surface. Return to your breath and acknowledge the truth that your body is a temple, an expression of the living Oneness.

Continue scanning your entire body. Begin with your feet and move slowly toward your head, observing and feeling each sensation: tingling, tension, energy, temperature, softness, pulsing, and so forth. Proceed slowly and examine each distinct part: your feet, ankles, calves, knees, thighs, pelvis, buttocks, belly, chest, back, shoulders, neck, and head. Give yourself time to complete this; it usually only takes ten minutes or so.

Assess your breathing. Is it deep or shallow? Fast or slow? Simply allow it to be. Pay attention to how your body responds to your breath: the rise and fall of your chest and belly, the air moving through your nostrils and throat, and your lungs pressing gently into your back. Become aware of your breath reaching all the way down to your feet. How does it feel there? In your hands? Your head?

Tune in to the subtleties of your body. Feel your heartbeat and relax into its simple, steady beat . . . the pulse of life that connects all things.

Now allow your body to rest in gentle awareness and loving compassion. Tap into the vibration, thought, and feeling of absolute love. You may first feel it in your toes, your eyes, or in your throat—wherever its origin, let it grow until it encompasses your entire being. Experience absolute, unconditional love. Feel everything—your cells, glands, bones, blood, and nervous system—vibrate to the frequency of love. Make this your intention now. Breathe love and compassion into your body temple. Allow it to move like a wave, cresting and falling. Feel the ecstasy of life and love flow through you. Bathe in this delight; feel the luminosity within you.

Pay attention to any area of your body that's speaking to you. It may be a part that feels tense or painful, or perhaps it feels warm and relaxed. Be fully present and listen for its wisdom and guidance, for your body holds a wealth of information and connects you with the deeper truth of Oneness. In Oneness, all aspects of life are expressions of the Divine that inspire and guide you—your body is an example of this truth.

Play with this practice throughout the day, especially when you feel tired, out of sorts, or disconnected. Within a few minutes of engaging in this, you can return to presence. Remember that your body can be used as an instrument of Oneness or of separation. Today, choose to focus your body temple as an expression of the living Oneness. Let it guide you into a deep, meaningful resonance and relationship with the world.

Affirmations

*I AM fully alive and thriving in this moment,
in tune with my body and the world.*

I AM a Divine temple, an expression of the living Oneness.

THE RESTORATION OF ONENESS

-

"God blessed the seventh day, and sanctified it: because that in it he had rested from all his work which God created and made."

— **Genesis 2:3**

"Emptiness is the pregnant void out of which all creation springs. But many of us fear emptiness. . . . We prefer to remain in the realm of form, surrounded by things we can see and touch, things we imagine are subject to our control."

— **Wayne Muller**

"There are thoughts which are prayers. There are moments when, whatever the posture of the body, the soul is on its knees."

— **Victor Hugo**

James: Why do we work ourselves to the bone, rarely, if ever, giving ourselves the rest and relaxation we need and deserve? Is it because a part of us doesn't want to let down its guard, as if being fully restored would open the door to other discoveries—other possibilities—that our ego doesn't want us to consider? If we hold still we'll find ourselves, and then we'll realize Oneness. But that can also be something we're very much afraid of. Why? Because it means we're far more responsible than we thought we were, not only for our own lives, but for the world we live in. Maybe allowing ourselves to be restored is one of the ways in which we experience Oneness.

Anakha: This has been a personal challenge for me: allowing myself sufficient time to rest and rejuvenate. I've noticed that when I don't, it pushes me deeper into the fear of not doing or being enough. The thought is usually that I need to constantly strive and be on the go, maintaining control and making things happen, instead of resting and letting myself experience the natural creative movement of my life. I've realized that the Divine flow that wants to move through me requires stillness.

The restoration of Oneness asks us to surrender and trust life, having faith that we are always supported, loved, and nourished. Rest and stillness often go against our culture's fast pace and sole focus on achievement, which has become the norm. Yet this obsessive striving for success often takes us out of the consciousness of Oneness. Relaxation and reflection are critical practices that allow us to open up and be receptive to something far greater than our limited minds might be able to perceive, conceive, and receive.

James: We've been told that the more we do, the more valuable we are. So there's this dichotomy that has been set up between doing and being. And over time it has been hammered into us that simply "being" is the equivalent of laziness. However, it's this precise state that allows us to open into our greater selves, helping us do more in the world. The more limited or restricted we are, the less we can really accomplish. If we allow ourselves to be restored—if we give ourselves the time to rest, meditate, and engage in whatever spiritual practices resonate with us—we can be more effective.

Gandhi once said that you must "be the change you want to see in the world." It's not just about talking or acting; it's about being it, feeling it, and allowing it to permeate your entire consciousness and life so that it's not you creating but Spirit acting through you. This is what it means to be an *instrument of peace.*

Anakha: Beautiful! Yes, in that place of contemplation, of resting in the presence of Oneness, there will be a natural inspired flow of guidance moving through us, which activates inspired actions that work for our own good and for the well-being of all who are connected to us. Restoration is crucial in order to receive the Divine inspiration that will bring blessings to the world.

Exercise

Today's practice is a return to the sacred rhythm of rest. Tuning in to your natural cycle includes attending to your needs for rest and relaxation. This, in turn, keeps you connected to Oneness and resonating with your life and the world.

For this moment, release the pressure to incessantly "do" and "produce"; and take the time necessary to root yourself in the beauty, abundance, and trustworthiness of this sacred universe. Give yourself permission to relax. Find a place where you can sit or lie down and just be. Rest is a holy practice. Repeat this to yourself: *There is nothing to do, nowhere to go . . . nothing, no thing. To be here now is enough; I am a blessing.* Relax and be in relationship with the All That Is. Breathe in. Breathe out. Sink into the arms of Oneness—the arms of love, of peace, of God. Imagine, feel, and know that you're being held by the universe. You are supported, nurtured, and rejuvenated.

Allow the sacred rhythm to restore balance to you and your relationships, to remind you of who you truly are and why you're here. Allow the Divine Presence to rekindle your creativity and your passion for life. Allow yourself to be tended to while you relax in the restoration of Oneness, held by the web of life. Rest, restore, and remember. Return to your center, knowing that you are both blessed and blessing. Give thanks for the wonder of it all.

Use this practice throughout the day to bring yourself into the awareness and presence of Oneness and restore your innate connection to Life. Right now, take 10 to 20 minutes to simply rest in Oneness.

Affirmation

I AM remembering who I AM, trusting the sacredness
of life as I rest and take refuge in the Oneness.

☞ PRACTICE 8 ☜

THE SOURCE OF ONENESS

"To discover joy is to return to a state
of oneness with the Universe."

— **Peggy Jenkins**

"Even Kings and emperors with heaps
of wealth and vast dominion cannot compare
with an ant filled with the love of God."

— **Guru Nānak**

"I, the fiery life of Divine Wisdom—
I ignite the beauty of the plains,
I sparkle the waters,
I burn in the sun, and the moon, and the stars."

— **Hildegard of Bingen**

James: We all have to come to terms with our concept of God. I say *concept* because that's how the ego thinks of it—as something that's easy to either accept or deny, not a real living entity we can experience and realize . . . well, that's something very different, something to avoid at all costs. If we don't, then we might fall into that reality and experience ourselves as One with it. Maybe this is why the great mystics preached that we're really One with God, while those who argue over theories and study theology prefer a God that is judgmental and something (or someone) to be feared.

What if we were to hold still and let the living God find us? What would happen then?

Anakha: Some of the most exciting and amazing questions we can ask ourselves are: *What is my relationship to the living God, the living Power and Presence of Oneness? What is the most intimate connection that I personally have with what might be called God, the Divine, or Source?* Our connection to the All That Is, in fact, is a unique experience for each of us. Everyone has their own relationship and way in which they experience God. For some it might be through nature, and for others it may be a flowering of the heart, a commitment to servitude, or in moments of play and laughter. And I think it's so important to discover what really ignites the Divine fire in our hearts, minds, and bodies. Whatever fans our internal flame—whatever brings us alive and ushers us into the sacred tremoring of life—this is what inspires us and unfolds the Oneness in our midst.

Ask yourself those vital questions. Your experience of Oneness may change from moment to moment, but you can always seek an expanded relationship to the Source of Oneness. You can continually ask: *How do I connect myself with that Source and allow myself to be infused with it and rooted in it?* To be rooted in Oneness and to grow from it is such a powerful experience.

James: We're constantly trying to limit God, which means we're really limiting ourselves because we're an extension of the Divine. We create religions and constructs, and proclaim: "This is the way!" or "That is not the way!" We build up ourselves and our ideologies to somehow prove we're right, yet *A Course in Miracles* reminds us to ask ourselves whether we'd rather be right or happy. I think that God desires our joy, not our "rightness." God prefers that we be happy and seek joyful experiences, rather than always having to be right about our concepts of God. So I think the more we stay open, the more accepting we can be of others and how they hold that Source we sometimes call God. Then we can gently yet powerfully move into the reality of the living God rather than just the theology of God.

Anakha: Many of the concepts and structures we hold around who or what God is are actually designed to keep us safe. They're born from the ego's fear. This is one of the reasons why the myriad religious constructs often clash and also why so many wars have been fought in the name of God—because often our rigid ideas the Divine are sourced in fear. So part of what we need to do is break down those walls and soften our understanding so that we can be more receptive to the living God right here, right now.

Thinking of our different perceptions of God reminds me of the story of the blind men and the elephant: one of the men was touching the elephant's tail and describing the creature in one way, and somebody else had hold of its ear and was describing it in another way. We're all receptacles of the living God. We must be receptive and open to learning from each other in order to expand our view so that it includes everyone's unique experience of the Divine.

Exercise

We are each connected to the inexhaustible source, the overflowing fountain of Oneness, the fiery love of God. We have many names for it, and we each have our own way of connecting and relating to it. Connecting to the Source of Oneness unleashes the stream of love and life so that it flows continuously through us.

Today's practice is a treasure hunt, an excursion into the source of Oneness. Allow yourself to uncover your unique relationship to it. Listen inwardly, for you know the truth: the universe is one living organism, with a single substance, a single heart, and a single Soul. Feel it, see it, and be moved by this dynamic and unified impulse. Let it take shape and form, color and image. How does it taste, what does it sound like, and how does it move? Allow the Source of Oneness to come to life. Watch the theater of life as it unfolds before you, and let it be a dynamic and ever-changing dance of Oneness.

As you move through your day, notice what catches your attention, what attracts and allures you. Let the Source of Oneness draw you to it. It could be a color, sound, movement, person, place, or an object—trust your impulses and intuition as you engage in this quest for your unique connection to Oneness. Be seduced, allured, and transformed by it.

Each night before going to bed, connect with the Source of Oneness that lives within your heart. Find the Divine spark, which silently and continually beckons you. It's the flame that illuminates the darkness and connects your Soul to all things. Remember that the Source of Oneness is within you and within all things, interwoven in a sacred bond that unites us.

Affirmation

I AM a dynamic expression of the living Oneness,
constantly changing, growing, and expanding.

THE BELONGING
OF ONENESS

"I am a living member of the great family of all souls."
— **William Ellery Channing**

*"It's the most precious thing . . .
to know absolutely where you belong."*
— **Tessie Naranjo**

*"The hunger to belong is not merely a desire to be attached to
something. It is rather sensing that great transformation and
discovery become possible when belonging is sheltered and true."*
— **John O'Donohue**

James: The desire to belong is one of our most basic needs. This is because the opposite (isolation) is too hard for us to bear: it would mean that we're alone or cast out. When we belong, we experience a sense of Oneness, whether it's within a group, a club, or our own families. When we "fit" somewhere, we feel safe, and this helps us discover who we really are.

I think the key is that we need to "belong" to ourselves first before we can belong to others—in other words, we must be at home in ourselves and not waiting around to gain acceptance from others. We all want to be friends with the individuals who have a healthy sense of themselves, who are comfortable in their own skin. And we naturally avoid those who have low self-esteem or who are resisting their own beingness. I believe we have to wholeheartedly accept ourselves; we have to belong to ourselves— embrace all parts of ourselves, including our shadow as well as our light. We need to know that both aspects make up who we are. It's not about pushing away the dark areas but integrating them so that we can be whole.

Anakha: Yes. This is part of our remembrance practice, recalling that we naturally do belong here, we belong to each other, and we belong to the one purpose that we're here to express on the planet. As soon as we start to question or think that we don't belong, it's a losing game because we move into ways of being outside of our nature in order to be accepted and feel a false sense of belonging. That never works!

Part of this practice is to genuinely remember your essential belonging—to yourself, to God, to your loved ones, and to the global community. You have to remember that your presence on Earth is purposeful; you wouldn't be here if you weren't meant to be, if you hadn't agreed to be!

As it says in *A Course in Miracles:* "You are here on purpose, and your only purpose is to love." And yes, each of us has a unique delivery system of the One Love—that is, we express and bring love into the world in many different ways. We just need to find what that is, and then combine it with our shared purpose, which is to express loving-kindness.

Exercise

We all want to belong. Deep in our core, we share a universal need to feel welcomed and loved. Every being on the planet shares this trait—no matter how deeply buried or disguised it may be. And at its root, belonging is about being seen and received and coming home.

Allow yourself to connect with your own desire to love and be loved. Breathe into the center of your longing and allow it to grow. Imagine that every person in your life—everyone in your community, town, city, state, and country—shares the same intensity and depth of longing. Allow this awareness to expand to include the entire world, and connect your longing to the longing of the world. This is a fundamental aspect of Oneness, your longing to be recognized and called home.

As you move through the day, gently hold this awareness of your innate belonging. Ground yourself in the truth that you're here on purpose. Feel the comfort, the kinship, and the passion that come from knowing you belong to the earth, and you're here to share your love with the world.

Notice the places and people with whom you feel a natural belonging as well as a sense of separation. Allow your love and compassion to encircle these experiences. Let it grow and expand.

How can you invite others to come home? Stay alert and watch for opportunities to extend the belonging of Oneness to your friends, families, co-workers, and even to people you don't know yet. Be inclusive and invite everyone. Open yourself, making the invisible web of life visible. Demonstrate the miracle of our interconnectedness. Meet this universal need by actively shining your light on the darkness of isolation and separation. Create a circle where no one is excluded, where all are invited to participate in the belonging of Oneness. Feel the love in your heart burst forth as you create a sense of deep belonging in, to, and with the world.

Affirmations

I AM included as an expression of Life,
embraced as an expression of love.

I AM here, I AM One, I AM home.
We are here, we are One, we are home.

☙ PRACTICE 10 ☙

THE SOUL OF ONENESS

"I am the self seated in the hearts of all beings."
— from **The Bhagavad Gita**

"The one thing in the world, of value, is the active soul."
— **Ralph Waldo Emerson**

*"The soul is made of love and must ever strive
to return to love. Therefore, it can never find rest nor
happiness in other things. It must lose itself in love."*
— **Mechthild of Magdeburg**

James: If the body is the symbol of separation, then the Soul has to be the opposite: the proof that we aren't separate and alone, but intimately linked . . . that we are One. When we live with Soul, we're living with vibrancy; and we begin to vibrate at higher levels. This is the goal: to live from the center of our being, the Soul that connects us with God and everything else we perceive.

Anakha: I think one of the key aspects of living a life from the Soul of Oneness is acting and moving with a deliberate sense of generosity . . . with a sense that there's not just "me" but "we." This means acting in the best interest of the whole—really seeking it and moving in a positive direction.

I'm reminded in my own life of areas where I feel the battle between my ego and Soul. The Soul is always wanting to move into connection, forgiveness, and compassion. But the ego wants to be right! It wants the other person to make the first move; it's like a cranky child who wants to be soothed and appeased. The Soul of Oneness extends love, but the shadow of Oneness is the part of us that wants to retreat in fear.

When we make the transition back into the Soul, we have to remember that we've been so conditioned to live from the ego that it may feel counterintuitive at first. We may be uncomfortable when we start to move into the generosity of the Soul, especially when we're feeling righteous or justified in our perception of a particular situation. We have to really be patient with ourselves and relax the grip of the ego so that the Soul can guide us back into meaningful and authentic connection. The Soul is always for Oneness; it will always open the door for us to reestablish that bond, while the ego demands that we stay "safe" and separate behind our carefully constructed walls.

James: There's a profound link between living with Soul and living in service. I think it's natural that when we open ourselves to Oneness, we want to help others. We genuinely hope to be of some benefit to the planet, and we want to share this state of Oneness. When we're living in the ego, we withhold our passionate energy because we're afraid of losing something that we think is valuable, that we may not have enough of. So I think it's important for us to remember that we have to keep giving and serving in order to continue that Divine flow in our own lives.

If we stop giving, we also stop receiving, and this isn't a one-time action. We don't just suddenly become enlightened and that's it. It's a choice we have to make in every moment, every day—and the way we do so is by staying in service. If we achieve this, our Soul remains the most active part of our lives, enabling us to live from that place in ordinary and extraordinary ways.

Anakha: Absolutely! And I love what you're saying about it being a moment-to-moment choice because in many ways, we're reprogramming our mind and way of being. This is a time of rewiring the world community to move from a place of fear and protection, of defense and attack, to a place of extension, expansion, and service so that love can flow. When love (Oneness) is adequately flowing, I believe that we'll live in collective abundance, a collective sufficiency. There may still be conflicts, but how they're resolved will be dramatically different when we're coming from a place of Soul rather than from the ego. Through our active embodiment and expression of Oneness, a true and sustained peace will be born in the world.

Exercise

At the center of the Soul of Oneness is unconditional love. It's the lifeline that connects us—the blood that courses through our veins. It's our most powerful, most abundant resource on the planet. And it's the fabric of our existence . . . it's who we are.

To experience the Soul of Oneness requires that you give the most precious gift you can offer others: your unconditional presence. When you embrace others with mindfulness and unabashed love, they bloom, thrive, and soar.

Begin your day by connecting to your own presence, the Soul of Oneness, through silence and prayer. Remember that you are *not* what you do, nor are you the various roles and activities that you may enact today. You're a Soul living in this human experience. Connect to your Soul with each breath. Fill yourself with God's profound love, allowing it to infuse your heart, your body, your mind, and your awareness. Know that in this present moment, and in every moment, you're connected to the Source of Oneness and are overflowing with compassion. When you take time to become present with yourself, you'll find that you naturally want to give the gift of your presence to others.

Practice being in this mind-set everywhere you go and with everyone you meet. Receive each person as a gift from God sent to you as a messenger and a reminder to be present. Extend your love to everyone. Listen beyond and between the words. Hear the expression of, and request for, love.

Today, your only purpose is to offer this most magnificent part of your own unguarded heart, your own unconditional presence. Treat each person you encounter as an extension of your Soul. Remember that often what is most precious hides itself—the wild and tender things have retreated and will only reveal themselves to those who are fully present.

Watch the preciousness unfold before you as you pay attention to what has heart and meaning . . . moment to moment, person to person. This is the Soul of Oneness.

Affirmation

I AM powerfully present, tending to the Soul of Oneness and offering my unconditional love to every person I meet.

THE EMBRACE
OF ONENESS

*"Embrace all things as part of the Harmonious
Oneness, and then you will begin to perceive it."*

— **Lao-tzu** (translated by Brian Walker)

*"Our task must be to free ourselves from this prison
by widening our circle of compassion to embrace all
living creatures and the whole of nature in its beauty."*

— **Albert Einstein**

*"Within us is an all-embracing light overflowing with
love from God that illuminates a divine path mysterious
and beautiful. If we acknowledge that light, we create
a new humanity of divine unity and everlasting bliss."*

— **Micheal Teal**

James: How passionately do we embrace life? Because of the ego's dominion, most of us hold back, hoping we'll be protected from having to make difficult decisions. We tend to welcome the experiences that are familiar and allow us to stay where we are, never attempting to leave our comfort zone or risk everything for the sake of achieving Oneness. Our ego wants us to stay put and trust what it shows us, but our Soul is far riskier. It doesn't gamble, however, because it knows where every difficult choice finally ends—with our personal evolution.

When we were going through growth spurts as teenagers, our knees ached from the dramatic, swift changes. Why should we be surprised when the same type of thing happens to us spiritually? After all, it's not easy to look at life in new ways even if it ultimately leads to enhanced levels of compassion and understanding.

Anakha: This practice is about inviting everything into our lives and into this field of Oneness that we've begun generating. I like this idea: that neither rejecting nor preferring any experience keeps us in that open receptivity. Like spiritual warriors, we're able to embrace everything we encounter, whether it's fear, despair, joy, or creativity. As Rumi says, "Welcome and entertain them all!" We must be open to all things so that we're able to expand and grow.

Author and spiritual teacher Debbie Ford sums it up nicely: "Are you willing to be uncomfortable for an hour a day, a month, or a year, if you knew that on the other side of that discomfort your life would be radically changed and transformed into something where you are experiencing more Oneness, more love, joy, peace, connectivity?" I really agree that when we walk this path of Oneness, we may be led into unfamiliar or uncomfortable territory, clearly outside of our comfort zone . . . and that's okay.

James: *A Course in Miracles* says that sometimes the things we think are best for us are really the worst, and the things we think are the worst for us are really the best. And this is why we must embrace all of it, no matter how it appears. We need to be grateful for everything that enters our path. In the tradition of the Desert

Fathers, there was a man named Abba Benjamin who said: "Be joyful at all times. Pray without ceasing and give thanks for all things." It's not just about being grateful for the easy and harmonious experiences in life, but about joyfully embracing all things, including the ones that challenge us. Confronting difficulties helps us go deeper into Oneness in ways we couldn't otherwise comprehend.

Anakha: One thing I'd love to add to what you've said, James, is that there are going to be times when we feel like our brains are being rewired. We have to let go of old ways of thinking and conceiving. In that process, we may feel disoriented and disconnected, simply because the neural connections in our brains are actually being rewired and refired. We have to be willing to go through that place of unknowing and of unlearning the concepts of separation so we can reconnect to the true knowing of Oneness.

Exercise

Today's practice invites you to fully embrace your life with naked, nonjudgmental awareness. The embrace of Oneness moves you beyond acceptance into a full and embodied experience of your emotions, sensations, and interactions in each moment. In the embrace of Oneness, you greet all things with open arms, ready and willing to be present with *what is.*

The practice begins by creating a "naked awareness" mind-set: a state of being where your mind is open, receptive, and non-judgmental—no rejection, no preferences. When you achieve this state, you're able to experience reality as it is, not as you would like it to be. Your transformation involves going from resistance and rigidity to deep openness and expansion, allowing the flow of Life to move through you.

This is the freedom that the embrace of Oneness offers you. It's a state of being, a place of presence where you discover your wholeness and the wholeness of life in each moment. This is the liberation from your enslavement to expectation and attachment, which are barriers to Oneness. In the embrace of Oneness, despair may be a precursor to unimaginable joy. And if you reject that despair, the joy is also suppressed. Oneness invites you to be in communion with what is and welcome the totality of your experiences with a compassionate and loving embrace.

This practice has no beginning and no end. It is fluid and depends upon your willingness to create a receptive embrace of the truth of your moment-to-moment experiences. It requires your willingness to see yourself as you truly are. Thus, the embrace of Oneness is a "dynamic" meditation, as it follows the ebb and flow of your life.

For today, be fully present and attain a calm and naked awareness of your surroundings. See life as a witness and a participant, exploring the dynamic relationship between the two. Notice any propensity to judge your emotions, sensations, or thoughts. When you do so, bring yourself back to a state of gentle awareness. Soften the hard edges of judgment with the breath of compassion. Allow yourself to ride the wave of your life with the grace and agility of a seasoned surfer.

Whenever you have difficulty openly accepting what is, breathe in and out, and whisper the words of the mystics: *All is well. In all matters of life, all is well.* Practice the following steps to tap into the embrace of Oneness and surrender to the natural flow of the river of life:

- Create a calm mind (a naked, nonjudgmental awareness), a sanctuary of unconditional presence.

- Use your breath to create the willingness to sense and feel the reality of your life.

- Lovingly embrace everything you encounter, be it joy or despair, grief or elation, agitation or harmony, confusion or clarity . . . allow *what is* to dynamically flow into the next *what is.*

- Remember that all is well. *In all matters of life, all is well. Amen.*

Affirmation

I AM lovingly embracing every experience of my life, which flows in dynamic surrender and in perfect beauty.

⌒ PRACTICE 12 ⌒

THE TEMPLE OF ONENESS

"Your daily life is your temple and your religion. When you enter into it take with you your all."

— Kahlil Gibran

"This is my simple religion. There is no need for temples; no need for complicated philosophy. Our own brain, our own heart is our temple; the philosophy is kindness."

— The Dalai Lama

"The moment I have realized God sitting in the temple of every human body, the moment I stand in reverence before every human being and see God in him—that moment I am free from bondage, everything that binds vanishes, and I am free."

— Swami Vivekananda

James: We've all heard the saying that our body is the temple of our Soul. That's a beautiful analogy, but what would happen if we expanded the idea to include everything else we perceive? What if we viewed the infinite aspects of nature, or even the people in our lives, as Divine temples? How would our lives change if we viewed the individuals we're having difficulties with as unique, amazing expressions of God?

All we have to do is acknowledge all the temples God created and respect them as whole and perfect. What a wonderful way to enter the experience of Oneness, especially when at times it can seem incomprehensible or too far away.

Anakha: I think what happens when we're in relationships with others and they're bringing something to our awareness that feels foreign to us, our tendency is to push it away, especially when it doesn't fit our understanding or perspective. If we can welcome each person—knowing that this is the face and voice of God speaking to us—we can then ask, "What is the Oneness trying to invite me into?" Instead of automatically rejecting or discrediting that voice of Oneness (no matter how it's arriving), we begin to understand that it has something to teach us. That requires a softening and an opening, as well as the willingness to truly listen to the voice of God, the voice of Oneness. Then we take the information and use it for our own spiritual awakening.

James: We've all been inside temples or churches that have been neglected or are in decay, and it's always sad to see such sacred places fall into ruin. And yet if the foundation is solid, it can always be raised again. When St. Francis set out on his journey, he began by rebuilding the churches around Assisi that were most in need of repair. But he was really rebuilding his own temple—his spiritual temple. He was re-creating his own life, and because *he* possessed a strong foundation, he was able to accomplish that task.

So what does our foundation look like? How do we go about rebuilding our own spiritual temple? If we have the courage to go inside—to be aware of the neglected corners and the spots that need cleaning—then we can enter this sacred task. And in doing so, we can experience Oneness to a much greater degree.

Exercise

What would it be like to feel at home wherever you go? At home in your body, in your relationships, in the world, and even in the universe? What if you could experience everything as holy and whole? What amounts of peace, freedom, and joy might that bring you? Today you're invited to experience everything and everyone you encounter as an integral aspect of the temple of Oneness. All are invited into this temple, and everything is contained within it. Nothing exists outside of the sacred temple of Oneness.

Begin this practice with a deep realization of your own wholeness. Remember that you're a sacred temple—home to the Divine, to Oneness, to Love. This is your true identity, your Soul's identity. You are a temple of Oneness. Know this, and become rooted in this truth. Emanate and radiate this essential wisdom: *I AM a temple of Oneness—home to God, a house of Love.* Allow the inner fire and light of this temple to grow and encompass your whole body. Feel the temple of Oneness surround you.

Now imagine this view expanding to include your home, neighborhood, and city—the traffic, the buildings, the people, the streets, the cars, and so forth. Imagine everything enveloped by the warm light that shines in the temple of Oneness. Expand your awareness again to include the state in which you live, your country, and eventually the entire planet. All sentient beings and all of nature are living in the temple of Oneness. Allow your experience to expand even further to include the universe. Explore every aspect of the temple. What lives within this holy sanctuary? Do you see children, animals, stars, plants, people, statues, oceans, rivers, mountains, buildings, and cars? What else? They are all living temples of Oneness.

Slowly allow your awareness to return to your own body. Feel the world and the cosmos contained within you. Sense the cells in your body, and know that each is an entire universe unto itself. Remember that you inhabit all of these temples of Oneness—from microcosm to macrocosm. There are many temples held in the *One* temple, as Jesus affirmed: "In my Father's house are many mansions."

Remember this as you walk in the world today. Look upon everyone and everything with the gaze of Oneness. This transforms the ordinary into the extraordinary. A tree, a cloud, a bicycle, a poster, a mini-mart, and a cat are all living temples of Oneness. With everything you encounter, ask yourself, *What does this temple of Oneness hold?*

Feel at home wherever you go. No place, person, or experience is foreign. Remember that all beings, all things, are Divine, integral parts of the expansion and expression of Oneness.

Affirmations

I AM awake, walking in the world.

I AM a holy temple of Oneness.

THE ELIXIR OF ONENESS

"Indeed, God hath created everywhere around this Gate oceans of divine elixir, tinged crimson with the essence of existence and vitalized through the animating power of the desired fruit."

— **The Bāb**

"By the elixir of divine love, the solar regions are strong; by the divine elixir, the earth is great; the divine elixir is stationed in the midst of all the constellations."

— from the **Atharvaveda**

"This nectar, trickling from the palate, is the sweetest of all tastes. Each drop is worth more than millions. This elixir will expel all your diseases and fill you with gladness. Your anger will vanish. You will exude ambrosial sweetness. You will rejoice in your spouse and children. As you taste this nectar and become absorbed in it, you will be transported with inner delight."

— **Swami Muktananda**

James: When Joseph Campbell first wrote and spoke about the "hero's journey," he described a very distinct path that can be found in all of the great stories throughout history, which describe our own spiritual journey. One of the most important elements we find in these archetypal legends is the hero bringing the "elixir" back to the ordinary world. Without this final turn, the story has no real value—that is, nothing has been learned or gained. So the question for us is: What elixir are we bringing back from our own hero's journey? Are we going to add to the misery we see everywhere we look, or can we bring back love and compassion, the natural gifts of an open heart?

The elixir of Oneness comes from our moment-to-moment acceptance of who we really are, then giving that gift to others. Another way we can describe this is Unconditional Love. This is the elixir that the world is waiting for right now.

Anakha: Throughout this dialogue, James, we've emphasized the phrase *moment to moment.* And I do think that ties back into the earlier practice of the rhythm of Oneness. The lived experience of Oneness is truly a moment-to-moment awareness and choice. The choice is whether or not we'll become *present to the Presence*— the constant awareness of unconditional love that is always flowing to us and within us . . . it's who we truly are.

We must ask ourselves: *What am I identifying with in each moment? Am I identifying with the truth that I am made in the image and likeness of Love, of God, of Oneness? Or am I identifying with the fear and separation of the ego?* And moment to moment, we get to choose how we're responding.

It really does require—if we're going to bring this elixir into our own bodies—that we walk the razor's edge with a "laser consciousness" about our moment-to-moment choices. Are we moving in the way of love and Oneness, or are we on the path of fear? Discerning these answers requires us to slow down and pay attention.

James: The elixir is in this moment. It's not in the past or future; it's right now. And it's only by living in this present moment that we accept the elixir into our life. The more we embrace it, the more it flows from us to the world . . . into our relationships and touching the people around us. But that can only come by being fully present, realizing that the gifts of God are given to us now, and that this is what the elixir of Oneness really is. It's realizing that in this moment, we can experience Oneness, and this will transform our lives.

Anakha: It's a constant tuning in to the field of absolute love, unconditional love . . . the elixir of Oneness.

Exercise

The elixir of Oneness is none other than the presence and power of unconditional love. It's the sweetness of *agape* (tender, benevolent affection and compassion) and the fire of Divine Love. It's the life force that animates and sustains all life. It stirs the consciousness of Oneness, allowing it to emerge, blossom, and bear fruit. It's what causes the rose to bloom and release the scent of the sacred.

Just like sap in a tree, the elixir of Oneness lives in your body: it swims in your blood, oscillates in your nervous system, and beats in your heart. There are many words for it—including Kundalini, Holy Spirit, Chi, Ka, Prana, Mana, Gtumo, The Microcosmic Orbit, and Shakti—all referring to the experience of the vital energy of love rising and circulating throughout your body, heart, mind, and consciousness. The elixir of Oneness awakens the evolutionary force within, growing in you as love.

Today's practice begins with tapping into the elixir of Oneness that's already alive and well within you. Sit or lie down in a comfortable position. Become aware of your breath, finding a pace and rhythm that feels most pleasurable and satisfying to you. Breathe in and out. Inhale sacred love, circulate sacred love, and exhale sacred love. Continue your breathing, circulating Divine love to all of the cells throughout your body. Allow your breath to tickle each limb and organ, every part of your being. Let it dance within you, nourishing you with its sweet ecstasy. *Inhale sacred love, circulate sacred love, and exhale sacred love.* Smile as you bathe and delight in your own life-force energy. Feel this course through your veins and vibrate in your cells, awakening this sleeping giant of life, love, and bliss.

Continue to allow the essential life-force energy to build and strengthen. Gently bring your attention to your heart chakra, the source of unconditional love and compassion. Allow the sacred energy to flood your heart with tender loving-kindness. Feel your heart soften and open, like the petals of a rose blossoming in the warmth of the sun. *Inhale sacred love, circulate sacred love, and exhale sacred love.* Allow the love in your heart to fan the Divine spark into a powerful flame.

Now turn your attention to your base chakras, which are the roots of your connection to the earth and the fountain of creativity and sexuality. Feel the potency of life force as it builds and activates within these centers. *Inhale sacred love, circulate sacred love, and exhale sacred love.* Acknowledge the beauty of your connection to nature and to all life. Experience the pleasure and ecstasy of your own creativity, sexuality, and sensuality as the elixir of Oneness brings you into aliveness, radiance, and presence. Let go and trust the presence of God, the universal life force, as it leads you into full resonance with the consciousness of Oneness. *Inhale sacred love, circulate sacred love, and exhale sacred love.*

Allow this life-force energy to move into your belly, into the navel and the solar plexus, stirring the fire within—strengthening your will to live, to create, to transform, and to be here now. Know that you have the ability to do anything you put your mind to. Permit the fire of unconditional love to fuse with the fire in your belly.

Breathe this energy through the heart, dedicating your connection, creativity, and personal will to serve your mission of love. Feel this vital energy expand and open your heart even more as it swirls and spirals throughout your entire being. Know that the sacred source of life force lives within you and that it can be activated through your conscious contact with it.

Continue to breathe this energy to your throat, the center of expression. Let it vibrate through your vocal cords and then shoot up into your third eye, the place of intuition and knowing. Let it vibrate in your head and up through your crown, shooting beyond to the heavens and then falling back down to bathe your entire being in the sweet elixir of Oneness.

Feel your whole body and being vibrate and resonate. Feel the hum of life force zoom through your cells. Feel alive and radiant; feel good; feel God. This is the experience of Love in the body. Bask in it, live in it, and create from it.

Make it your intention to live within the awareness of and in connection to this vital energy every day. Allow everything you experience to bring you alive. Imagine and know that everything is conspiring to love you and wake up your life-force energy. Use everything to feed, nourish, and strengthen you, from the water you drink and the food you eat, to the colors you see and the air you breathe. Vibrate, tremor, and dance. Come alive with the ecstasy of life, for this is the elixir of Oneness.

Affirmation

I AM opening to the greatest Mystery of all,
becoming Love's alchemy realized.

THE SENSATION OF ONENESS

"And forget not that the earth delights to feel your bare feet and the winds long to play with your hair."

— **Kahlil Gibran**

"The greatest gift of a garden is the restoration of the five senses."

— **Hanna Rion**

"Our senses are indeed our doors and windows on this world, in a very real sense the key to the unlocking of meaning and the wellspring of creativity."

— **Jean Houston**

James: Take a sip of really good wine but don't swallow it right away. Let it rest on your tongue a little longer than you're used to. Really experience the texture and flavors; and think about all the work that went into the grape harvest, the process of fermentation, and even the bottling. What did it take to get that amazing taste sensation into your glass, then into your body? Try this with a great cup of coffee, too. How do you feel afterward?

These are the moments we usually miss because we're so preoccupied with getting to the end of a journey rather than the journey itself. But what would happen if we used the *sensations* we experience in everyday life to enter a state of Oneness and union?

Anakha: Oftentimes we use the spiritual journey to attempt to escape and hide from being in the body and in relationship with the world. When we go into a transcendent state, the spiritual landscape can be so beautiful, so amazing, that it becomes difficult to return to the body and experience the grit, chaos, and messiness of everyday life.

The practice of the sensation of Oneness is really about resacralizing (making sacred once again) our senses in order to be fully present in the here-and-now. We bring Oneness into the moment through touching, tasting, seeing, hearing, and smelling; and as we connect with these sensations, we dwell in the temple of Oneness. We begin to experience our relationships and our lives united with our transcendent awareness of Oneness and as something that we can actually embody and experience moment to moment. We do that through the practice of tuning in to our senses, breathing in and feeling the Divine life force moving through us.

James: There's such a fine balance between allowing the sensations to transform us and realizing that we aren't actually the bodies we believe ourselves to be. Both of these realizations have to happen at the same time. On the one hand, we can't use this to escape from our bodies; we need to bring all of those sensations inward and be aware of them in order to be fully present. And if we can do that, then there's a transcendence that takes place that helps us realize we're free—in other words, we aren't bound to our body . . . we are Souls having a human experience.

I think that the power of all of these lessons is that they trigger the moment-to-moment presence as well as this transcendence, which, when combined, catapults us into a state that is so unlike anything we've ever experienced. It's what St. Paul might call the "peace that surpasses understanding." It's not something we can "get" in our minds, but an understanding that we only compre- hend within our Souls. I believe that this is the key to Oneness.

Anakha: Oneness invites us into the "both/and," the "third way"—not using spiritual practice or mysticism to escape from the world or our bodies, but using it to embrace both as an experience of Oneness. We begin to realize that it's not an "either/or"; in fact, there's tremendous power and creativity in the fusion of the two.

Exercise

Your senses are a doorway to Oneness. They take you straight into presence and the core of your original nature. They ground you in the reality of your innate connection to and resonance with life. You are a sensing being, and this is a sensing universe. Becoming present to your five senses, as well as your sixth sense, restores your natural mind-set of undifferentiated unity you were born with.

In today's practice, you'll use your senses to connect with the oceanic field and feeling of Oneness, the shared foundation of humanity. Celebrate your senses as you smell, taste, touch, see, hear, and know the ground of Oneness. You can use this practice as a morning or evening meditation and to heighten your aware- ness to the sensation of Oneness throughout the day.

Begin by taking several deep, full breaths. Become still and present to this precious moment. Breathe yourself into a calm, open, and centered state of mind; and engage in the following steps:

1. *Open to the sense of sight.* Fully see what's around you. Take in the colors, textures, shapes, and movements. What do you notice? Expand your vision so that you see the details as well as the larger picture of life as it unfolds. Let everything you perceive feed and enhance your vision. Open to the gift of sight as a doorway into Oneness.

2. *Open to the sense of smell.* Breathe in the air and life around you. Open your nose to the scent of life. What do you smell? Experiment with this. Sniff the blanket on your bed, roses in a vase, your lover's shirt, an orange, a tree, the earth, your own skin. Inhale the fragrance of life around you. What scents are most pleasing to you? Open to the gift of smell as a doorway into Oneness.

3. *Open to the sense of touch.* Touch the life around you. Feel the textures with your fingertips. Reach out and touch the Oneness. What do you feel? Experience the sensation of Oneness using your feet, hands, cheeks, toes, and so on. Immerse yourself in the sensation of touch and discover a new world. Allow your sense of touch to be enhanced by the textures that touch you. Open to the gift of touch as a doorway into Oneness.

4. *Open to the sense of hearing.* Listen to the sounds around you. Open your ears to the symphony of life calling to you. Hear the sound of Oneness. Can you describe it? Listen to the sounds and the silence. Experiment with making your own sounds. Tune in to your inner and outer ear, and experience the orchestra of life serenading you. Allow your sense of hearing to be enhanced by the sounds around you. Open to the gift of hearing as a doorway into Oneness.

5. *Open to the sense of taste.* Taste the flavors of life around you. Open your taste buds to the flavors of Oneness. Savor everything you eat and drink. What do you taste? Experiment with the sensation—taste air, water, fruit, skin, and sunshine. What does love taste like to you? Open up and taste life! Open to the gift of taste as a doorway into Oneness.

6. *Open to the sense of knowing.* Experience the knowing that lives beyond your five senses. Feel the knowing of Oneness. What do you perceive? What lies beyond your knowing? Experiment with your sixth sense—your intuition and unique perception—and let it guide you to Oneness. Allow your knowing to be enhanced through your conscious contact with your intuition and Divine guidance. Open to the gift of knowing as a doorway into Oneness.

Now that your sight, smell, touch, hearing, taste, and knowing are activated, allow them to move together in a sensory dance of Oneness. Experience your connection to life through your six senses, as this is the sensation of Oneness.

Affirmation

I AM unlocking the meaning of life, living my connection to the whole through the wondrous sensations that surround me.

THE TOUCH OF ONENESS

"At the touch of love, everyone becomes a poet."
— **Plato**

"Touch seems to be as essential as sunlight."
— **Diane Ackerman**

"Some men know that a light touch of the tongue, running from a woman's toes to her ears, lingering in the softest way possible in various places in between, given often enough and sincerely enough, would add immeasurably to world peace."
— **Marianne Williamson**

James: What would happen if you let this day be an opportunity for touching and really feeling the ordinary things in your life? For example, if you walk to work every day, perhaps there's a tree that you pass over and over, but you've never actually touched it. Make time and do so today, and really feel the connection you share.

How about the people in your life? How can you touch them (appropriately, of course) in a way that expresses the love in your heart? You can even try reaching out to them without making any physical contact; in other words, make a connection that is more essential, one that comes from your Soul. What would happen if you realized all of the opportunities you have to touch others today, and then allow yourself to be touched in the process?

Anakha: I think this is one of our longings and also one of our fears, especially in America and other Western cultures. It's being afraid of touching each other, which is ultimately the fear of intimacy, of being seen and known. It also carries out in actual physical touch. Just like a newborn requires loving touch in order to grow emotionally and mentally into the fullness of what he or she is meant to be, we also require it. We respond and open in the presence of loving touch.

As we allow ourselves to take in the experience of touching and being touched by the world, we feel more alive and radiant. We find that we thrive just by sensing the touch of a breeze, the sun, or a tree; and we start to be *in relationship* with life as we're experiencing it here on Earth, instead of being numb to it. As one of my friends says, the problem isn't global *warming,* it's global *numbing.* We've become detached and indifferent not only in heart, but also in our ability to connect to each other—physically, emotionally, and spiritually.

Exercise

As you become increasingly conscious of your breath, you'll become aware that your body isn't limited by your skin—in other words, it surpasses your physical sense of touch. This is the touch of Oneness. Your skin represents about 16 percent of your body, and it's the most sensitive organ, the one that nourishes you the most. Allowing yourself to touch and be touched by the world inspires creativity and is the embodiment of Oneness.

Allow yourself to be caressed by a tree, kissed by a flower, and supported by a rock. Reach out and run your hands over the bricks of a building. Cup the rain in your hands. With presence and grace, experience the Divine touch of Oneness.

To touch another person in this way necessitates being the other person, and to achieve this, you must live in a state of Oneness. In this practice, you're invited to move beyond the illusion of separation of the body into deep connection with all of life around you.

As soon as you wake up in the morning, become conscious of your skin—the soft, thin membrane that holds and protects you. What sensations do you feel? Warmth, well-being, ease? As you rise, notice the change in temperature. How does your skin react? Feel the contact of your feet on the floor, your hand on the door, and your body as it moves through the room. Notice the different textures and temperatures as you shower, dress, eat, and prepare for your day. Water, soap, sponge. Fabric, leather, hair. Bread, apple, knife. Be fully present with everything you touch, absorbing the wondrous sensations on your skin.

Throughout the day, your skin will change environments and respond to all kinds of stimulation. This continuous tremor and radiance will bring your awareness into the embodied experience of Oneness. Trust your body and your presence, and have faith in your desire to touch and be touched by life.

Experiment by touching with deep reverence. Touch others as if you were touching yourself. Reach out with the intention to love and be loved. Know that this is a sacred gift of Oneness: when you touch others, you're being touched as well, which restores the body to its sacred vibration. Acknowledge your fears and relax in the knowing that this is an essential aspect of achieving Oneness.

Allow yourself to view your skin as an instrument of love, enabling you to be truly present. This is the touch of Oneness.

Affirmation

I AM tremoring with the textures of life, nurturing and nourishing the loving touch of Oneness.

THE SEEDS OF ONENESS

"We plant seeds that will flower as results in our lives, so best to remove the weeds of anger, avarice, envy, and doubt, that peace and abundance may manifest for all."

— **Dorothy Day**

"Whatever we do lays a seed in our deepest consciousness, and one day that seed will grow."

— **Sakyong Mipham**

"Whether you tend a garden or not, you are the gardener of your own being, the seed of your destiny."

— **The Findhorn Community**

James: Our lives are like gardens. We're always planting seeds, but we usually forget about them and are later astounded by the harvest. When we plant seeds of suspicion and fear, we're often surprised when they bear fruit in the future. Maybe the key is to be aware when we're tending our garden and know that everything we put in the soil will return to us. It may not happen today or tomorrow, but in the end, the gifts we offer are the gifts we receive. It takes consciousness to live in harmony, and this is what leads to our experience of Oneness.

What would happen if we decided to plant just one seed instead of so many? What if we consciously planted love and compassion in every situation? Is that what would return to us? If we realized that life is a garden, we also acknowledge that our thoughts are the seeds that lead to either Soul satisfaction or ego delusion. The choice, as always, is ours.

Anakha: If we want these Oneness lessons to radically transform our experience of life on a day-to-day basis, we have to practice them daily. This is a Oneness workout! We're building our "muscles" by actually doing the practice of cultivating and planting the seeds that will grow and blossom into the lived consciousness of Oneness. This takes a vigilant awareness of what we're planting. Are we planting seeds of humility, compassion, forgiveness, love, and gratitude? Or are we planting seeds of fear, lack, separation, resistance, and conflict? Minute by minute, we get to choose what we're putting into the sacred soil of our being, knowing that whatever we plant will blossom, manifesting the conditions of our lives.

Just as an athlete prepares for the Olympics, we're spiritual athletes preparing for an embodied and lived Oneness. It takes training and exercising those muscles, especially the ones that might not be very well developed. What might those lesser-developed muscles be? Personally for me, I've been focusing on tenderness, extending compassion to others. I'm a fierce truth teller, and I've been building up my muscles of tenderness and compassion with equal gusto.

James: I'm glad you brought this up because consistency is the key to success. If we plant seeds of compassion and peace one day and that's it, it's like throwing one seed into the earth and forgetting about it. We're not going to have an abundant harvest; we may end up with just one plant (if we're lucky).

We speak so much about abundance and how we want to experience the richness of life. If that's true, we have to be consistent about which seeds we plant. We have to be planting seeds of compassion and peace every day, and when those seeds begin to sprout, we have an entire field of possibility. This is what happens when we keep returning to this idea of moment-to-moment Oneness.

Anakha: You're reminding me to see the full picture—that is, our inner garden. We don't just buy seeds and start planting them right away. First, we must till the soil. Then we remove the weeds and rocks so the earth will be receptive to those seeds and they can flourish. And that's really what these practices are designed to do: we're preparing the soil of our being so that once the seeds of Oneness are planted and nurtured, they will grow and blossom into the conditions of our own lives and ultimately the conditions of the world.

Exercise

Sowing seeds of Oneness requires you to grow the garden of your heart. Your heart holds the precious seeds of Oneness. Many of these are already growing and manifesting as the conditions of your life, and others may be waiting for your conscious attention to activate them. For the seeds of Oneness to eventually blossom and bear fruit, they need to be nurtured by your willingness to cultivate Oneness and to conform your nature to that of the Divine. *Your Divine nature is the nature of Oneness.*

Today's practice requires devotion and discipline. In the book of Galatians, it says: "The fruit of the Spirit is love, joy, peace, patience, kindness, goodness, faithfulness, gentleness, and self-

control; against such things there is no law." Other seeds of Oneness that we must plant include compassion, tenderness, selfless
service, nonviolence, inclusiveness, receptivity, gratitude, surrender, devotion, and generosity.

Today, cultivate the soil in the garden of your heart by actively
devoting yourself to embodying Oneness. Dedicate yourself to
being a living, breathing expression of the qualities of Oneness.
Consciously demonstrate these traits in everything you do. Nur-
ture and grow them by planting seeds of Oneness every day. Create
a garden that lifts, inspires, comforts, and heals everyone around
you. Through your conscious intention, you're creating the outer
conditions of your life via the inner cultivation of the seeds of
Oneness.

Reflect on the following questions in quiet contemplation or
by journaling at the beginning of your day:

1. What kinds of seeds do I want to grow in my garden—
    the ones that will blossom into the outer conditions of
    my life, my community, and my world?

2. What seed of Oneness will I devote myself to planting
    today?

3. How can I demonstrate my commitment to this seed
    of Oneness in both consciousness and action?

4. What support do I need from God to sow this seed in
    all that I am and all that I do?

Now imagine yourself planting this seed of Oneness in your
heart, watering it, nurturing it, and watching it grow. Write the
name of it on a piece of paper, and keep it in your pocket or on
your desk or dashboard. Center yourself with it, using the name
as a mantra and living prayer throughout your day. In all situations and experiences, return your focus to cultivating this seed
of Oneness. Invite others to join you in planting and growing the

garden of Oneness. Through your devotion and discipline, *you* are becoming a glorious, blossoming garden. These are the seeds of Oneness.

Affirmation

I AM a blessed seed of Oneness flowering in the heart of humanity.

⟣ PRACTICE 17 ⟣

THE BLOSSOMING
OF ONENESS

*"The most precious gift we can offer others
is our presence. When our mindfulness embraces
those we love, they will bloom like flowers."*

— **Thich Nhat Hanh**

*"And the day came when the risk to remain tight in
a bud was more painful than the risk it took to blossom."*

— **Anaïs Nin**

"Earth laughs in flowers."

— **Ralph Waldo Emerson**

James: We have a choice to make today: what kind of flowers do we wish to grow, and to what degree will we choose to enjoy them? We already know that we reap what we sow, and the seeds we plant today produce tomorrow's harvest. But what about the flowers? They blossom and produce such beautiful patterns, feeding us in ways that other plants cannot. It may not be food we can eat, but it nurtures us nonetheless.

Consider buying some flowers for yourself today, and pick out really special ones—in other words, treat yourself to types that you may not otherwise consider. Then spend some time just gazing at them, and perhaps think about what they had to go through to produce the blossom you're enjoying so much. What did *you* have to go through for your life to blossom? These are the questions that lead to the experience of Oneness.

Anakha: I love the image of fully bloomed flowers that began as the seeds we planted from moment to moment! One of the things that's most exciting for me to consider is the vision of the full opening of Oneness in the world. When we as sacred activists, spiritual peacemakers, and extraordinary human beings begin to embrace these practices and realize this Oneness in our lives and relationships, the very fabric of the world tapestry will change from one based in fear and separation to one that's rooted in love and unity.

And this blossoming spreads and creates a ripple effect . . . a tsunami of Oneness that effortlessly sweeps through the collective consciousness of separation. Many of us have been cultivating these seeds, attempting to manifest this for quite a while, and it feels like the time is finally ripe! The blossoming of Oneness can actually envelop, infuse, and impact all areas of darkness and separation, not only in our own consciousness and lives, but also in the greater consciousness of the world.

James: Exactly. I think we're witnessing the blossoming of a global consciousness more profoundly than we ever have before. One of the things that has triggered this is all of the adversity we've been experiencing in our lives and around the world. But without those struggles and challenges, we can't blossom into a new stage of evolution.

We'd like to believe that evolution takes place in gentle ways, in gradual steps, but that's never how it happens. A piece of coal becomes a diamond when tremendous heat and compression are applied. Likewise, when fire and pressure are applied to our lives, it forces us into a new state of being. It also spreads, and an undeniable and unstoppable momentum begins to build. This is what we're seeing now—an all-powerful force that's leading more and more Souls into the state of Oneness. And as more Souls accept that state of Oneness, it becomes not only accessible to other people, but inevitable.

Anakha: I love how these practices tie together and reinforce each other. As we embrace Oneness, we're welcoming even the things that feel difficult. This is also analogous to the sand irritating the oyster in order to create the pearl and the effort of the seed to push its way up through the dark, heavy, damp earth. I'm guessing that the seed is pretty tired of its own spiritual practice (of trying to reach the sun) by the time it finally bursts out into a young sprout! In this practice, we're invited to embrace everything in ourselves and in our world and use that raw material to fuel and feed our blossoming into Oneness.

Exercise

Today, take time to stop and smell the roses, literally and symbolically. You've been consciously tending to your garden of Oneness through disciplined and devoted practice. Now it's time to take a moment to reflect and examine. What's growing in your garden? Is anything blossoming and bearing fruit? How is the ever-blooming consciousness of Oneness changing you, your relationships, and your life? Acknowledge yourself for your decision to become a spiritual gardener, sowing the seeds of Oneness . . . seeds of love, connection, and union.

Notice how Oneness is unfolding in your Soul. What unique qualities of Soul are growing in your life? These emit fragrances in the form of a spiritual personality, creating an atmosphere of grace and carrying the aroma of the sacred, of Oneness. What scent are you offering to others and the world?

Spend time with a blossom today. Look for one in nature or treat yourself to a majestic rose, joyful tulip, luscious peony, or whatever calls to you. Be in prayerful communion. Imagine that this blossom is an outward expression of the inner flowering of your heart as a mystic, lover, and peacemaker in the world. Notice its colors, textures, and scent. What are its qualities? What qualities do you share with it? What guidance and inspiration does this blossom have to offer you on your journey into Oneness? What does it inspire you to become?

Allow yourself to overflow with the joy, beauty, and infectious delight of this flower. This is the blossoming of Oneness.

Affirmation

I AM the scent of the sacred emanating the perfume of Oneness.

THE CREATIVITY OF ONENESS

"I want creation to penetrate you with so much admiration that wherever you go, the least plant may bring you the clear remembrance of the Creator."

— **St. Basil the Great**

"God is really only another artist. He invented the giraffe, the elephant, and the cat. He has no real style. He just keeps on trying other things."

— **Pablo Picasso**

"You become more divine as you become more creative. All the religions of the world have said God is the creator. I don't know whether he is the creator or not, but one thing I know: the more creative you become, the more godly you become."

— **Osho**

James: Who can you inspire today? Several people probably come to mind, those you deal with every day in the most ordinary fashions . . . the ones you could choose to give the gifts you're seeking in order to receive yourself. How can you change the predictable patterns that you usually follow in ways that may inspire something new? Remember that the best way for you to receive inspiration is to offer it to someone else. Can you be creative today? Can you offer something that helps another person access Oneness and also inspires the same in you?

Anakha: Yes! I think the creativity of Oneness is so necessary right now. We have to realize that who we were yesterday isn't who we are today. We must move out of those fixed ideas of ourselves and what the state of the world is. It's much more dynamic than that! In the creativity of Oneness, each day we become new—that is, there's a new aspect of Oneness that's actually expressing itself as us and as our friends, family, co-workers . . . even as this very world. As we become fluid and flexible, allowing ourselves to be infused with the Divine Intelligence that wants to speak to us, through us, and as us, we become part of a global consciousness, a global community of Oneness.

It's important to be receptive to an intelligence that's so far greater than our limited minds, to be open to it and to activate it in ourselves and each other. We need to encourage one another to be available to the Divine Idea of Oneness that wants to manifest in our lives and as the conditions of the world.

James: When I think about the word *creative,* or *creativity,* I also think of *compelling.* To be creative is to be compelling. This is something that's so vital today, especially if we want to inspire others. This needs to be compelling! We can't be somber, and we can't just lie back and relax into a passive state. If we can live this mind-set in creative, vibrant, passionate ways, then people will look at us and say, "I want some of that!" This is how we can be inspiring in the world today: by stepping into that experience ourselves, living it, and embracing it fully so that others will desire it and access it for themselves.

Anakha: Yes. I think that the passivity you're speaking of (you can also call it malaise) is like a cloud that gets in the way of the sun's brilliance. We have to make it our intention to connect with the power of the sun—the power of Oneness and creativity. It's easy to become complacent and collectively depressed about the state of the world instead of realizing that there *is* a God idea, a Divine idea that we can tap into. And it's our duty and responsibility to actually make ourselves receptive to Divine inspiration and to also encourage others to do the same. That's how dynamic, creative ideas for our educational and political systems, the economy, the environment, and new ways of living together on the planet today become manifest: through our receptivity to them.

Exercise

The creativity of Oneness is constantly calling to you. Now is the time to answer the call and open yourself to the boundless inspiration available to you. When you hear the Divine knocking, fling the door wide open and invite your own particular genius inside. When you do so, you become receptive to the creativity of Oneness. You're filled with wisdom and enthusiasm that is deeply and intricately connected to your well-being and to the well-being of the world. This inspiration is sourced in the Divine Idea of goodness for all. The creativity of Oneness taps into the collective Soul and delivers to your doorstep a notion of life that surpasses your wildest dreams. Your creativity fans the flame of Oneness; this is the Divine spark that connects you to the Source of all life.

Today, notice which Divine Ideas catch your attention and intention. What do you want to create? Do you feel pulled toward something? What fascinates you or whets your appetite? If you were to stop conforming to someone else's idea of creativity, how would you express your own unique brilliance? Would you dance, paint, cook, sing, garden, act, draw, write, dress up, decorate, orchestrate, or design? Trust the Divine impulse that moves you to express and contribute. Have faith and act. As the wave of creativity rises and swells within, catch it and ride it in! This is the creativity of Oneness at work in you.

As you increase your willingness and ability to receive, conceive, and act on Divine inspiration, you open the channel for more to flow through. Divine inspiration for all aspects of your life will become easily accessible to you. Have the courage to create today! Make it contagious. Invite others to join you, uniting in the creativity of Oneness.

Take out a pen and paper. Set your watch or a timer for seven to ten minutes, and begin to write in a stream-of-consciousness style, allowing the words to flow uninterrupted onto the page. In other words, don't stop or edit. Don't think. Just go with whatever naturally arises. You may write the phrase *This is so stupid!* 30 times before something fresh comes forth. Trust the process and *go.* Create!

To get your engine purring and the words flowing, here are several jump-start phrases. Pick one of the following and jot it down on the top of a blank piece of paper or in your journal. Then start writing! Whenever you feel blocked or want to dive deeper, rewrite the phrase and continue to let your thoughts flow freely. Have fun!

Jump-start Phrases

Who am I	Can you see me
Behind my eyes	Innocence
What matters	Alone and together
What I see	Why am I here
In my strength	What I really want
What I know	Becoming me
Lost and found	Waking up
What is true	Going deep
In my hopes	Sometimes
What is real	Underneath
What I remember	Who I used to be
What I want the world to know	Inside my mind
The truth about me	If only
What if	Being the truth
Finding my way	What draws me to it
In the silence	What's growing inside me
Where possibility lives	Inner voices
Inside out	Honoring myself
Finding my voice	When I'm there
A window into me	Who lives inside of me
Who will I be	What I'm afraid of
In the center of myself	By myself
What changes everything	Locked away
In the mirror	Finding the key

Affirmation

I AM consciously creating a world of brilliance and Oneness with my every expression—prayer, thought, statement, feeling, and action.

THE SPONTANEITY OF ONENESS

"Only in spontaneity can we be who we truly are."
— **John McLaughlin**

"Play is the only way the highest intelligence of humankind can unfold."
— **Joseph Chilton Pearce**

"I still get wildly enthusiastic about little things. . . . I play with leaves. I skip down the street and run against the wind."
— **Leo F. Buscaglia**

James: The ego thrives on predictability in every situation, while the Soul seeks spontaneity. How can you be more spontaneous in ways that challenge you? It's easy to stick to a routine and avoid leaving your comfort zone, but what would happen, for example, if you overcame your fear of looking like a fool and sang a silly song as loud as you could on a busy street corner? Maybe it would open something new inside you—something that needs to wake up. Today is the day for risk taking because you're never going to experience Oneness unless you let go of the ego's fear of appearing foolish.

Anakha: Yes, and this practice creates a more unbound self, one who is free to be fully alive. We can be free because we're supported. We can sense Oneness affirming *Yes!* Yes to life, yes to love, yes to this grand experiment, yes to play, and yes to the chances of looking like a fool for God's sake! This is the Sacred Yes factor!

If we really think about it, we often realize how serious we've become. We've limited the ways in which we express ourselves. Yet when we experience Oneness, feeling it in our bodies and in our lives, we start to possess suppleness and an ability to respond moment to moment without deep contemplation. When we live within Oneness, we act in more natural, open, and even childlike ways, more in tune with curiosity, play, and fun.

I believe that this is necessary medicine in our world today—especially for those of us who are spiritual practitioners and seekers. Bringing the levity of Oneness into our daily lives can help it truly blossom and bear fruit.

James: The greatest mystics were usually also known as "fools" for God. They weren't bound by the ego's constraints; rather, they entered the flow of life in spontaneous ways. As long as they were expressing their passion for Divinity and Oneness, it wasn't important what other people thought.

If we can manifest that same passion, if we can find ways to live spontaneously, then we can be a powerful inspiration to those who are locked in their own minds and egos. Most people are afraid to reach out and stretch beyond their normal boundaries. These are the walls we've created in our minds . . . nowhere else. But the truth of who we are was created by the Divine, by God. It's in choosing to live in that holy creation that this spontaneity flows and brings us into a deep state of Oneness.

Anakha: I love that. I'm reminded of one of the core teachings of Jesus: *Be in the world but not of the world.* We take this consciousness—this spontaneity of Oneness—into the world, and we inspire a whole new way of being. In many ways, we're going against the grain, against the common views of society, when we're truly connected to and following the spontaneity of Oneness.

Exercise

Tuning in to the reality of Oneness connects you to wholeness, innocence, and to the natural rhythm of life. From this, deep trust and surrender are born. The outward expression manifests as childlike joy and freedom in the now. In the spontaneity of Oneness, you become moved, animated, inspired, and illuminated by life. You are connected to the bubbling fountain, the effervescent Source; and your life becomes an expression of beauty, play, and flow. In the deeply rooted knowing of your Oneness, you have faith and are able to let go of your ego. Fear and resistance dissolve, and you're free to swim in the warm and inviting sea of life. Play, laughter, fun, and creativity are all expressions of the spontaneity of Oneness.

Give yourself permission to live in this mind-set today. Go beyond the routine of your scheduled tasks and habitual actions, and explore the realm of childlike wonder. Feel and follow the fluidity of inspiration and impulse, allowing it to sweep you away. Let go and be alive within this free-flowing and continuous state of clarity and joy. Be fully present and open to whatever arrives in each moment. In this pure, vibrating consciousness, all sense of separation will dissolve. It's the simple, essential truth of Divine love . . . the spontaneity of Oneness. Relax in total immersion in the Divine, and follow the invitation of your Soul.

One of the signs of a life sourced in the spontaneity of Oneness is experiencing Soul grandeur. Yet you may wonder how you can attain this in your modern life—in a culture that often cuts you off from communion with your natural mysticism and sense of wonder. French philosopher Gaston Bachelard, the author of *The Poetics of Space,* asserts that three factors are required for living a life of spontaneity and passion: intensity, intimacy, and immensity. Allow these qualities to become your guides today as the universe sweeps you away in its natural rhythm and flow.

— **Intensity.** St. Thomas Aquinas said that zeal comes from an intense experience of the beauty of things. How would you describe these "intense experiences" of your life? Do you feel like you're being pulled toward something unfamiliar that will perhaps vanquish the illusion of boredom once and for all? What fans your inner flame? Go directly to that experience right now! Don't delay or distract yourself from the intensity of life that beckons you, for it is here that you'll come face-to-face with a living Oneness that will bathe you in radiance and bring you to life.

— **Intimacy.** Andrew Harvey said, "In every tradition, the Presence is [said to be] hungry to reveal itself and to enter into ecstatic and intimate communion with its own creation." God exerts a continuous attraction on your heart, pulling you, in love, toward God. Today, allow yourself to experience the joyful ecstasy of being gently drawn to your Eternal Beloved. Pay attention to what your heart is longing to experience and express. What will bring you into intimate and ecstatic communion with yourself, with life, with others, and with God? Let yourself be drawn like a moth to the flame to whatever your heart and Soul are longing to experience. Dare to be intimate with yourself, with others, and with God in the spontaneity of Oneness.

— **Immensity.** Psalm 139 states: "Where can I go from your Spirit? Where can I flee from your presence? If I go up to the heavens, you are there. If I make my bed in the depths, you are there. If I rise on the wings of the dawn, if I settle on the far side of the sea, even there your hand will guide me, your right hand will hold me fast." Allow yourself to fall in love with the stars, the planets, and with all Life today. Fall in love with the immensity of life and return to elemental awe! Feel your connection to the primordial sense of being, knowing that you were birthed from the cosmos. You are wondrously and magnificently made—*Imago Dei*—in the image and likeness of God. Allow yourself to follow what naturally connects you to the awe-inspiring majesty of life, of the world, and the entire universe. Be willing to be swept away in the spontaneity of Oneness.

Affirmations

*I AM living a life of Soul grandeur, a life full
of intensity, intimacy, and immensity.*

I AM flowing with the spontaneity of Oneness.

⌒ PRACTICE 20 ⌒

THE DESIRE OF ONENESS

"Bliss becomes blissful with practice. In our own bliss the desire, desirer and process of desiring are united—they are one. Desire is fulfilled at its source."

— **Maharishi Mahesh Yogi**

*"People who renounce desires
often turn, suddenly,
into hypocrites!"*

— **Rumi** (translated by Coleman Barks)

"Desire is the very essence of man."

— **Benedict de Spinoza**

James: Oneness is something you have to desire with your whole heart and Soul. If you want it just a little bit, or in ways that aren't too challenging, you'll never achieve it. This analogy sums it up nicely: A wise teacher once held his disciple's head underwater until he almost drowned. When he released him, he asked the student what he'd been thinking about. The student replied that the only thought in his mind was getting a breath of air. The teacher responded: "When you want God like you wanted that breath of air, then it will be yours."

Ask yourself the same question today: *What do I most desire?*

Anakha: This practice is so important, for it cuts straight to the heart of Oneness. However, we're often programmed *not* to be connected to the energy of our desire. We fear and mistrust our own longings, and other people's, yet authentic desire takes us into the field of Oneness where we welcome and accept everything. Desire is actually one of the energies of our Divine life force. Therefore, it's essential that as we go out and create a world based in Oneness, we actually trust and follow our innermost longing and authentic desire. When we do so, we become connected to others who possess the same mind-set. And in that, the possibility for creativity and blessings is magnified and multiplied.

If we aren't trusting ourselves or if we're unwilling to become aware of our innermost desires, we block the blossoming of Oneness in our lives. In this manner, we remain detached. The invitation of this practice is to become present to what fuels our lives and connects us in perfect harmony to others who have similar desires so that we can work together in powerful new ways.

James: One of the Buddha's primary teachings is the principle of "desirelessness." I'm not sure if I can personally accomplish that or not. To me, it makes more sense to be aware of what I desire and then ask God how I can use it to achieve the most good. When our desires are turned toward service, they become more than just extensions of our ego; they're extensions of our Soul, bringing us closer to the state of Oneness.

So for me, this isn't about being desireless; it's about realizing from moment to moment what I'm wishing for and determining if the seed of Oneness is within it. If it is, I ask how it can be shared with others. Then it takes root in ways I couldn't have ever imagined, inspiring me and others . . . and sometimes even changing the world.

Anakha: It's important to differentiate between what may be compulsive or addictive behavior (which is distraction, not desire) and the Soul's authentic desire (which is naturally rooted in Oneness and will bless all). Many times we find ourselves out of harmony with the natural desires that are rooted in God, in our essence. We ignore them, and that actually makes us feel grumpy, "off," and depleted. This is because we're creating unhealthy soil of separation rather than cultivating nurturing, juicy soil where the seeds of Oneness can be planted. It's crucial to honor our desires, especially when they come from our sincere, deep knowing within.

I think that recognizing the desire of Oneness is very simple. The energy of obsessively trying to reach for something outside of ourselves has a different quality to it than the natural feeling of our inner longing. We can begin to trust the longings that are seeded in Oneness and follow them as they blossom.

Exercise

Trust your innate desires, sourced in the presence of Oneness, to bring you into profound connection with yourself, others, and your Divine purpose. Your authentic desire is one of your most precious and vital life-force energies; it's essential in order to achieve lasting fulfillment and well-being. Allowing yourself to trust and follow your heartfelt wishes is a powerful practice of Oneness. Everything proceeds from this state, and no single action or thing is more worthy than another. As you follow your inner wisdom, you play an essential part in creating a world that benefits everyone, that blesses all.

Enter into the resonant field of the desire of Oneness and know for certain that it exists in you as it does in all things. In Oneness, you'll discover a universality of desire and enter into its radiant and luminous space. In fact, cosmologist and scientist Brian Swimme tells us: "By pursuing your allurements, you help bind the universe together. The unity of the world rests on the pursuit of passion." Are you willing to pursue your passion in order to manifest the energy of Oneness in your life and the world?

If your answer is *yes,* then the willingness to be wholly available to life is all that's necessary to enter into this practice. What passions will you discover? Where will life take you as you follow the energy of desire in every moment?

By following your longings, you'll find that true presence to life offers you incomparable happiness. The simplest things, such as drinking a hot cup of tea, relaxing in a warm bath, and staring into a crisp blue sky can bring you tremendous delight as long as you're present to it. In other words, you can discover absolute joy simply by being aware of and fully embracing the ordinary experiences of life. You'll become free from needing intense experiences in order to generate desire and pleasure, and you'll be enlivened and enthused by pure existence and your relationship to it in each moment.

Nothing and no one can take away the desire of Oneness and the beauty, peace, and bliss it offers. It is yours as you become present to it. Your full presence and receptivity to desire creates a powerful medicine that will begin healing the schism between your body and mind, your ego and Soul.

Today's practice requires nothing more than your desire to be wholly available to life. What amazing things will you discover amid the seemingly mundane activities in your life today? If you decide to practice the desire of Oneness 60 times a day for 15 seconds, you'll spend 15 minutes simply *being.* For today, 5 minutes will suffice.

Become present, feeling the energy of desire and allowing yourself to receive the blessings each moment carries as it unfolds. Find the delight and joy in simply recognizing this awareness. Feel the Divine radiance of life bringing you into a deeper relationship with yourself, your essential nature. Breathe and be in relationship to all things: the clothes you're wearing, the food you're eating, the sidewalk you're walking on, the hand you're shaking, the music you're listening to, and so forth. Love each moment through the desire of Oneness.

Whenever you feel disconnected and experience a schism of the body and mind, the Soul and the ego, return to presence and feel the desire of Oneness unite and restore you. For today, give yourself permission to experience the excitement and allure of the desire of Oneness. Spread your passion for a life of Oneness!

Affirmation

I AM living the fullness of my Soul's desires in each moment, forever bonded with the world in the passion of Oneness.

Dialogue on Practices 21–30

James: There are shadows within us that wait for us to abandon our spiritual quest and return to our comfortable old ways. But when we commit to a practice like this, it stirs the water, and we're suddenly able to sense all of our limitations, all the shadows we're holding on to, because we're afraid we may not survive without them. This is natural, and it's not something to run away from. Instead, we should run toward our shadows because they'll ultimately lead us to healing and Oneness. That's the purpose of the next series of lessons: to embrace the fears that may be rising within and learn how to integrate these teachings on even deeper levels.

Anakha: I'm relieved that we're opening ourselves to this territory: the dark and shadowy spaces, the places where we're still fearful and feeling constricted . . . not having fully healed into the reality of Oneness. A merely "espoused" Oneness—one that we believe mentally or spiritually but haven't applied in our daily lives—creates a split within us. It's important to acknowledge that we're all here on this planet in "Earth school"; and part of our curriculum is to engage in a spiritual practice that creates strength, resiliency, and courage so that we can face our shadows with clarity and integrity.

We need to engage in practices that enable us to bring the penetrating gaze of Oneness to those places of darkness, where we experience what I call *savior moments*. In such a moment, we say, "I, on my own accord, cannot release myself from this prison of separation, but through these practices and through my surrender to a higher power—to the Divine, to God—these places can be restored to Oneness." This is a natural and necessary part of the journey into Oneness: to examine, embrace, heal, surrender, and transform all areas of darkness and separation.

THE SHADOW OF ONENESS

"All beauty contains darkness."

— **Daniel Odier**

*"You cannot cause a shadow to disappear by trying
to fight it, by stamping on it, by railing against it, or by
any other form of emotional or physical resistance. In order
to cause a shadow to disappear, you must shine light on it."*

— **Shakti Gawain**

*"One does not become enlightened by imagining
figures of light, but by making the darkness conscious."*

— **Carl Jung**

James: When you stand outside on a sunny day, you cast a shadow on the ground. It's pointless to try to escape it, and running from it does nothing at all since it follows you wherever you go. Attempting to dodge your spiritual shadow is just as unproductive. You can turn away from it and pretend it's not there, but no matter what you do to avoid it, it's always right behind you. The only way to experience Oneness is to become a fully integrated being, and that means you need to embrace your light *and* dark sides. Your shadow has valuable lessons it can teach you, but you must be brave enough to face it.

Anakha: These dark and constricted places release a gift of Oneness when they're healed and transformed. There's an insight, an awareness, a part of our own brilliance that has been trapped in fear. So the good news is that once we're willing to actually face those areas (where we feel separation, judgment, or hold grievances) and shine the light of love and invite the presence of God and our higher selves to free them, we're also able to see the gifts.

We might discover an aspect of our wholeness that up until now has been suppressed because we weren't ready to look at those dark areas. But once we do, something is always revealed—an integral part of ourselves that had been concealed is called home to be integrated. This is the journey into embodied Oneness—the reclaiming of our innate wholeness, our true selves.

James: And once healed, our shadows become our strength and gift to the world. I like how you explained the concept, Anakha. We can also compare it to someone who has an addiction but confronts it and uses it as a way to serve others, to help heal people who have similar problems. I think these can actually become our greatest gifts.

We usually want to fall back into the traits of the ego, believing they make us stronger, yet there's a difference. "Grandiosity" is the gift of the ego, whereas "grandeur" is the gift of the Soul. Service enables us to discover our highest nature, but to be grandiose means that we puff ourselves up, and this is always the result of an unintegrated shadow.

When we embrace our darkness and allow it to heal, we feel stronger and wish to share our knowledge with the world. And this is, of course, one of the greatest aspects of Oneness.

Exercise

In Goethe's words: "Where there is much light, the shadow is deep." Today's practice is the first in a series of ten that will guide and support your descent into the shadow of Oneness. In your movement toward an expanded consciousness of Oneness, the opposite experience has most likely appeared. This is none other than the shadow of Oneness, which creates a mood of "unlove" and separation. These are areas within your psyche and life that are constricted and potentially frozen in fear, judgment, lack, limitation, or grievance. However, they're being presented to you now for transformation: for mending, healing, purification, and integration. This is a natural and crucial part of the journey. In fact, the awareness of the shadow is one of the primary intentions in order to heal and liberate those aspects of your being.

When your personal *Oneness Curriculum* appears, it's certainly time for celebration, for the Divine is taking you at your word. And through your disciplined presence and practice, the possibility for true and lasting transformation and illumination is at hand.

Today's practice requires that you find 45 to 60 minutes to become still, open, and reflective. Find a quiet room where you can begin this sacred journey into your shadow. Bring a candle, a journal, a pen, and a glass of water with you. Your intention is to make the darkness within you conscious. Facing your shadow and realizing the ways it reflects the collective shadow are important. Commit to doing so with trust, humility, and surrender; and you'll soon discover another level of unconditional compassion for yourself and the world.

In the shadow of Oneness, you'll discover that the very things that have threatened your sanity ensure your liberation. This is where the poison you've been ingesting becomes the medicine that will heal you. This is your salvation and return to wholeness—the great alchemy into which you are plunged.

Begin your practice today by taking several deep and cleansing breaths. Light a candle with the intention of viewing your shadow with the full power, presence, and tenderness of God. Do so with clarity, courage, and compassion. Spend several minutes in prayerful silence, reflecting on the following passage by Jesus from the Gospel of Thomas: "If you bring forth what is within you, what you bring forth will save you. If you do not bring forth what is within you, what you do not bring forth will destroy you."

Take out your journal or several pieces of paper. Ask for Divine guidance to assist you in bringing your personal "shadow of Oneness curriculum" to the surface. Reflect and write brief responses and notations to the following questions:

1. What core fears and limiting beliefs keep me isolated from the good that's here for me?

2. What are my most painful and harsh judgments about myself, others, and the world?

3. What grievances am I holding against myself, others, and the world?

4. Where am I sowing seeds of darkness and separation?

5. What am I now ready to acknowledge about myself that I haven't been willing to see before?

6. How are my own inner war and terrorism reflected in outer wars and acts of terrorism in the world?

7. What is ready to be healed and restored in Oneness?

8. What darkness needs to be illuminated so I can live my life in greater wholeness and in living Oneness?

Allow your answers to arise in your consciousness with grace and ease. Trust and accept everything with compassion. Practice *maitrī*—the Sanskrit world meaning "unconditional friendship with oneself." Breathe in and out, and accept yourself unconditionally. Write down enough information so that you can use it in future practices.

For today, your only need is to allow all insights to present themselves. Deeply trust this process. Have faith that the Divine will show you what needs to transform and heal. Pay attention to your life, for the clues are right in front of you. Everything you need to know about your shadow is appearing now: within your conflicts, your relationships, your struggles, and your judgments. Be willing to look and see. Be willing to embrace all aspects of yourself. Be willing to live a life of wholeness and Oneness.

Affirmation

*I AM entering the shadow of Oneness with courage and clarity,
shining light on the lost and forgotten parts of my being.*

THE FEAR OF ONENESS

*"Death is not the biggest fear we have; our biggest
fear is taking the risk to be alive—the risk to
be alive and express what we really are."*

— **Don Miguel Ruiz**

*"Our deepest fear is not that we are inadequate. Our
deepest fear is that we are powerful beyond measure. . . .
And as we let our own light shine, we unconsciously give other
people permission to do the same. As we are liberated from
our fear, our presence automatically liberates others."*

— **Marianne Williamson**

*"'What is love?'
'The total absence of fear,' said the Master.
'What is it we fear?'
'Love,' said the Master."*

— **Anthony de Mello**

James: It may sound insane to say that we're afraid of Oneness, but it's absolutely true. It would be the same as saying that we're afraid of God since God is the ultimate source of Oneness. We want to believe that the Divine is the last thing we would find frightening, but the phrase *the fear of God* is so deeply embedded in our consciousness that we forget it's even there. We're terrified by Oneness because we're convinced that it's necessary to give up something—specifically, our own selves. But this isn't accurate because we're already contained within All That Is (otherwise known as God). There's *nothing* to give up or sacrifice, so there really isn't anything to be afraid of. If we could only embrace this, then Oneness would fall in all around us without any effort at all.

Anakha: This fear is also about not trusting our innate wholeness and goodness. We think we have to keep ourselves protected from dissolving into Oneness, but it's just as Jesus said: only when we lose our lives will we gain our lives. It's only when we surrender and allow ourselves to be transformed by Oneness—and touched by others and the world—that we can discover our essential nature. This is the gift we each have to offer.

James: Of course, the opposite of fear is love, and love is always the result of dissolving into Oneness. So our fear isn't something to run away from; it's something for us to turn toward with compassion. And when we do so, we realize that all the negative thoughts, limiting beliefs, and "monsters" we perceived around us are only in our mind—that is, they're aspects of unhealed and unintegrated shadows.

If we can see them for what they are, they become detached from us and dissolve, and we enter the space of Oneness where we know that there's nothing to fear. There's only love, and it's drawing us deeper into the mystery of Oneness itself.

Anakha: I think we also need to touch on the fear of what might happen when our hearts start to break open. We need to open wide to our connections with our families, our communities, and our brothers and sisters around the world. We find ourselves becoming more compassionate, which makes us more sensitive to grief, despair, and violence. This can be frightening and over-whelming, for we often think we have enough to deal with in our own lives . . . connecting to the experiences of other people on the planet can seem like too much to take on.

However, if (coming from the place of Oneness) we can truly tap into that despair, grief, or hopelessness (the separation that many people endure today), we can use it to break our hearts open; and we'll experience an even greater capacity for love. And this will inspire us to follow our "heartbreak" into benevolent, sacred service.

Exercise

There is a collective fear of Oneness: the notion of being con-sumed or of losing one's identity, personality, and security. It is a fear of intimacy and being vulnerable, and ultimately a fear of death.

This belief system often presents itself in your close relation-ships. You're afraid to surrender to Oneness because you may "lose" yourself, when, in fact, quite the opposite is true. It's only when you're willing to lose your life that you receive your life. No aspect of your authentic self will disappear or be lost. On the contrary, your greatest self will be resurrected, illuminated by the journey into Oneness.

The fear of Oneness can also be experienced as powerlessness—the feeling that you'll be overwhelmed by the despair and violence taking place in the world today. On the path of Oneness, however, you'll learn ways to use this collective grief to open your heart and mind to even deeper states of compassion, love, generosity, and inspiration.

This practice begins with your conscious choice and intention to become aware of the ways in which your subconscious appre-hension drives your decisions and behaviors. Dedicate this day to actively transforming your fears by choosing to become present to them.

Allow the continuous background dialogue of insecurity and judgment in your mind to reveal itself to your gentle awareness. Listen carefully, as it has been influencing many of your choices and actions. At any moment, more than 90 percent of your actions are subconscious! Today's practice focuses on making your subconscious mind conscious.

As you move through your day, notice when you experience that inner dialogue—your harsh assessments and criticisms of yourself and others. Notice the tension and anxiety in your body, and the constriction of breath in your chest. These are the symptoms of fear and separation. As you spot these signposts, become present to them through your breath. Breathe in, breathe out. Engage in radical compassion and unconditional acceptance of yourself and others. Breathe in, breathe out, and gently notice.

This practice develops your *inner witness* and *wise mind*. Your inner witness has the capacity to observe your fears, and your wise mind can restore your thoughts to love so that you resonate with Oneness. Become aware of your fears by activating your inner witness today, for once your disquiet is revealed, you'll be healed. Tune in to your wise mind and return to a state of love, acceptance, and compassion. Remember to practice the Buddhist art of *maitrī* (unconditional friendship with yourself). Be gentle with yourself, as most of your deepest fears originated when you were just a child—fed to you by the adults around you who were themselves trapped by their own fear and separation.

Your willingness to face the fear of Oneness with conscious awareness and courage contributes to healing the intergenerational dysfunction of the world. Acknowledge yourself for your willingness to be an instrument of love. Dedicate your personal transformation to the transformation of the world. Use your personal sphere of awareness today as you actively reveal and heal your fears. To do so, become present in the here-and-now through these five zones of personal awareness:

1. **Sensing.** What are you sensing? What are you experiencing in your body? Use all of your senses to bring yourself into the present moment. Ask yourself, *What am I seeing, hearing, touching, smelling, tasting, and knowing right now?* What signals is your body sending you?

2. **Feeling.** What are you feeling? Become present to the shifting landscape of your emotions throughout the day. When you're anxious or apprehensive, face your feelings and ask yourself what this experience can teach you. What information about your core fears does it hold for you?

3. **Thinking.** What's on your mind? What are your judgments, opinions, assessments, and ideas? Become present to your thinking. Notice and jot down any fears or criticisms that consistently present themselves. They are your greatest teachers, for their resolution will guide you to freedom and wholeness.

4. **Wanting.** What are you longing for? What are your desires? Your needs? Become present to your wants, and notice that they're surrounded by your own trepidation. What does this reveal to you about your long-held judgments and fears?

5. **Acting.** What are your intentions? What action are you taking? Is it sourced in fear or love? Become aware of your actions today. Is fear dictating your movements, or does love guide your steps?

Affirmation

I AM healing the separation in the world through the transformation of my own shadow and fear.

THE HEARTBREAK OF ONENESS

"The deeper that sorrow carves into your being, the more joy you can contain."

— **Kahlil Gibran**

"The worst prison would be a closed heart."

— **Pope John Paul II**

"Those who are willing to be vulnerable move among mysteries."

— **Theodore Roethke**

James: God can easily enter a broken heart. When our hearts break, cracks allow the Divine to slip through, and then our hearts expand so that they contain even more love than before. The problem is that heartbreak is seen as a devastating experience— something to avoid, not run toward. But if we're really living our lives with passion and commitment, getting our hearts broken now and then is inevitable.

We can't hide from life just because we don't want to feel any pain. We also can't turn away from the very thing that unites us in compassion with the suffering of humanity. If we could just remember that the heartbreak of Oneness allows us to fully enter the mystery of the Divine, we wouldn't be so afraid of it.

Anakha: I think that as we allow ourselves to be pierced by Oneness (by love), as well as by anguish, we discover that the heart is one of the most powerful instruments of service. It is resilient and has an amazing capacity to endure and persevere. It's our fear that causes us to experience so much pain. When our hearts are expanding in shared heartbreak, we find power in the presence of God (or Oneness or love) that's available to us. We realize that we can bring this Divine power into any situation in our lives or into the lives of others.

We'll be surprised and delighted by what a gift the heart becomes when we really allow ourselves to undergo this opening.

James: One of the things we notice in the lives of the great mystics is that they weren't afraid. In fact, they threw their arms around every experience because they found such sweetness at the center of it all. I think this is the key to the heartbreak of Oneness: it takes us away from the outer crust of our lives to the very center, which is what unites us. If we look at the "outer crust" of all the different religious paths, we see the various dogmas and ways they're dissimilar. Yet if we allow ourselves to dive deep into any one of them, we find that the core is always the same—the heart of love and compassion.

I believe that this is really why it's so important for us to embrace all aspects of our lives—including heartbreak and suffering—because they can be the greatest gifts in helping us experience the deep passion of Oneness.

Anakha: Joseph Campbell told us to follow our bliss. And it might be said that we've created the world as it is by following our own personal agenda. Yet when we "break open" to Oneness, we discover a sense of belonging and our Divine purpose. Breaking our hearts open allows us to crack the mystery so that we can know for certain why we're here.

Exercise

When you open yourself to the bliss of Oneness, you also open yourself to heartbreak. You open yourself to feeling and experiencing the grief, terror, fear, and despair of others. You become aware of your intimate connection to situations, places, and people in your life (and in the world) who are crying out for your love, presence, and service. Following the heartbreak of Oneness will lead you to the dark and constricted places and to the people who need your light. *They are calling for the healing salve of Divine Love.*

Today's practice takes you into the heart of sacred service— devoted action born from the heartbreak of Oneness. What pierces your heart with love? What conditions of the world are calling you to greater levels of compassion and propelling you into sacred action? What heartache have you been numbing?

Allow yourself to look upon your world today with the heartbreak of Oneness. See the world as it is—both its light and dark elements. Become aware of the places, people, and events that cause you anguish; and permit your heart to break open through your unguarded awareness and presence. What "medicine" can you offer? How can you help others heal? One of the secrets to living in Oneness is to serve it. When your heart breaks open in Oneness, the question becomes: *How can I serve?*

Take a few deep breaths and settle into your body. Acknowledge the heartbreak you feel when you reflect on the conditions of the world. What calls to your heart and catches its attention? Scan your awareness, and feel the pain and suffering of others. Breathe in the energy of this separation, darkness, or constriction through your heart with the intention of completely accepting and owning it. Then breathe out, radiating loving-kindness and freshness—anything that encourages relaxation and openness.

Continue to breathe deeply. Feel yourself being opened in love to the heartbreak of Oneness. Feel this energy, and let your attention rest in it. Allow compassion, empathy, and love to build from the inside of your heart. Truly embrace the emotions of the heartbreak of Oneness. The intention of today's practice can be summed up in one word: *feel!*

The heartbreak of Oneness calls upon your deep integrity to serve the planet. The Divine invites you to wake up to and touch the grief, despair, and hunger in the world. Don't be afraid. Answer the call for help, and offer your medicine to the world in service to Oneness.

Take a few more deep breaths. Feel your heart radiating compassion, and express the profound love that moves through you. This is the heartbreak of Oneness.

Affirmation

I AM feeling my heart break open as I look upon the world with tenderness and compassion.

THE GRIEVANCE OF ONENESS

"All blame is a waste of time. No matter how much fault you find with another, and regardless of how much you blame him, it will not change you."

— **Dr. Wayne W. Dyer**

"One can spend a lifetime assigning blame, finding the cause 'out there' for all the troubles that exist. Contrast this with the 'responsible attitude' of confronting the situation, bad or good, and instead of asking, 'What caused the trouble? Who was to blame?' asking 'How can I handle this present situation to make the most of it? What can I salvage here?'"

— **Abraham Maslow**

"You are flawed, you are stuck in old patterns, you become carried away with yourself. Indeed you are quite impossible in many ways. And still, you are beautiful beyond measure. For the core of what you are is fashioned out of love, that potent blend of openness, warmth, and clear, transparent presence."

— **John Welwood**

James: It's time for us to lay down our swords and release the grievances that have kept us trapped in the illusion of separation. It's strange to think that our judgments about ourselves and others are the very things that keep us from experiencing Oneness. To judge another person means that we're seeing them outside of ourselves, separate and different from the concepts we have about who we are. We hold on to our grievances because they justify this separation and make us feel righteous. But at what cost?

Wouldn't it be better to lay all that aside and simply accept the truth that we need compassion and understanding, and that by giving it to another we also receive it? It may sound hard to do, but once we become accustomed to the freedom it brings, we realize that it's the easiest thing in the world.

Anakha: I think that one of the ways the grievances against ourselves, each other, and the world are created is through our own limiting beliefs and fears. When we feel threatened that something is challenging our worth, our security, or our goodness, we often manifest some "bad other" to project that pain onto, assigning blame to someone or something outside of ourselves. If we look at the world today, or even our own lives, we see that the places where we're experiencing the most conflict are the ones where we've created some sort of hardship or injustice in order to alleviate the pain of our own fears and sense of unworthiness.

As we commit to this path of Oneness, we need to examine how we're contributing to the outer turmoil in the world through the grievances we're harboring internally. Where do we make up stories about a "bad other"? When do we falsely elevate ourselves in order to alleviate our own suffering?

It takes real courage to become aware of our grievances and begin to offer them to the Divine for healing. It requires a sincere commitment to withdraw the energy we're putting into that hardship and instead sit with the pain. Yet as we endure it, those fears and old beliefs can't withstand the presence and all-loving gaze of Oneness, and they will eventually dissolve.

James: Among my favorite authors is a Jesuit priest named Anthony de Mello, and one of his greatest teachings was when he reversed the old saying, "I'm okay, you're okay," and said instead, "I'm an ass, you're an ass." I've always loved that because it instantly allows us to be more compassionate and acknowledge that we all have issues . . . we're all asses sometimes.

I can't embrace you until I embrace myself. And I can't embrace myself unless I'm willing to embrace you—it goes both ways. So when we realize that we're all enrolled in this "Earth school" (as you mentioned earlier, Anakha) to learn, expand, and heal, then we begin to set aside our complaints, our need to always be right. We begin to embrace ourselves and others in ways that offer healing instead of greater separation.

Anakha: What's coming to mind is that the withdrawal of grievances requires our ultimate vulnerability, our ability to be comfortable in our nakedness to ourselves and others. We must open up without reservation and declare: *Yes, this is a part of who I am. I entertain these thoughts, yet I am willing to release them as well.*

Exercise

In the ego's nightmare, other people and events in the world are feared and judged as unsafe. The ego's mantra is that the universe is malevolent. If there's good to be had, we have to compete and engage the "survival of the fittest" mentality to get it. This is the ego's game of win-lose, which ultimately results in total loss.

If you allow your grievance to control you, you engage in the losing battle of constantly perceiving threats and attacking. Your actions, choices, and behaviors reflect this illusion; and you begin operating in a world of separation. You create stories about the "bad others" to assign blame and relieve the pain of your isolation. In the journey into Oneness, however, all of your grievances are revealed for what they are. It's your choice whether to surrender the nightmare of your self-created separation for healing or to continue to suffer in the darkness.

Today's practice invites you to become aware of and identify your core grievances that operate in your life. Bringing your issues into consciousness enables you to free yourself of them. Most often these old beliefs have become your personal story. They're so deeply embedded that you mistakenly assume that they hold truths about you and the world. This practice helps you become aware of these grievances and deconstruct the stories you've created to support them.

To begin, think of something in your life that's painful, difficult, stressful, or consistently and persistently "stuck." You may want to consider your current relationships with your spouse, lover, friends, or colleagues. Consider other key areas of your life such as your health, finances, career, or even other relationships. When you think of a specific situation, what emotions, sensations, and thoughts arise?

When you engage the energy of your grievances, you set yourself in opposition to others and the world. How have you created a "bad other" in this situation or experience? What evidence have you collected, and what story have you created to ensure that your beliefs are legitimate? Allow yourself to become fully present by paying attention to your feelings and physical sensations.

Now ask yourself what feels familiar about this particular situation. Where or when have you felt this before? How does it relate to past experiences? How would you put this into words? Take out your journal, and start writing down your feelings in clear and simple statements: *You don't respect me. You don't appreciate and include me. You don't love me. You don't reward me. You don't want me. You don't acknowledge me.* Notice how your grievance taps into your core fears of feeling unworthy or unloved. Most of the negativity we project onto others and into the world is created from these limiting beliefs.

Now become fully present without harboring any blame or judgment. From this perspective, how do you think your grievances impact your life, your relationships? How do they contribute to the collective mood of separation in the world today? Take a moment to circulate your breath throughout your body. Breathe in, breathe out, and let go. Continue to take your own personal inventory, bringing your awareness to the grievances you harbor. Allow them to be transformed by your willingness to recognize, name, and ultimately and prayerfully release them.

Affirmation

I AM surrendering my grievances to the healing power of Divine Love and choosing the miracle of Oneness.

THE CRUCIBLE
OF ONENESS

"Lord, lock me up in the deepest depths of your heart; and then, holding me there, burn me, purify me, set me on fire, sublimate me, till I become utterly what you would have me be."

— **Pierre Teilhard de Chardin**

"Alchemy is the art of manipulating life, and consciousness in matter, to help it evolve, or to solve problems of inner disharmonies."

— **Jean Dubuis**

"The time has come to turn your heart into a temple of fire. Your essence is gold hidden in dust. To reveal its splendor you need to burn in the fire of love."

— **Rumi**

James: The key to experiencing our Divine nature is to completely surrender ourselves to the crucible of Oneness. It may be the hardest thing we've ever done because the ego believes that surrendering is the same as failing, which is unacceptable. What the ego doesn't realize is that it has already failed simply because it has tried to replace God's will with its own, and that is impossible. This may seem to be occurring at first, but in the end, nothing has been achieved.

So we must be on the path of surrender. We have to stop trying to control what we can't understand in our mind because our Soul already comprehends everything. This is the gift that Oneness offers us.

Anakha: I'm thinking of the story in the Bible about the lame man at the pool of Bethesda. He'd been paralyzed for 38 years, and one day Jesus appeared before him and asked if he was *willing* to be healed. In the crucible of Oneness, the Divine is asking the same of us because we're unable to really heal our fears and limitations on our own.

In many ways, our reptilian mind is so automatic. Our ego lives in the subconscious, below our awareness, yet it's actually driving our actions and behaviors. We can't heal ourselves through our conscious will. Instead, we have to get to the point of total surrender where we say: "Yes, God, I'm willing to offer all that I am—my brilliance and light, my darkness and constriction—in order to heal and transform." Apart from that, we don't have to do much else. We do need to identify what aspects of ourselves should be offered and then surrender, saying, "I'm willing to receive a full healing. I'm open to an expanded experience of Oneness and wholeness."

We think that we'd say yes to this automatically, but we don't because our transformation process is oftentimes very slow. I've heard that the difference between ourselves and the mystics is that these wise ones, when presented with an opportunity to transform and heal, would wholeheartedly and without hesitation agree to it. We, on the other hand, often hold back, saying things like: "Yes, but it better not cost me this relationship" or "It better not take too long or deplete my bank account." Yet when we finally embrace the crucible of Oneness, we affirm that we're willing to let everything go, and we're purified and brought into union with the Divine and our true nature.

James: We have to ask for help; we have to request our own healing. This is why surrender is so important. We can't do this on our own, and that's okay. Entering the crucible requires that we dissolve and merge with all of the other elements. We must allow ourselves to be "stirred," to be changed. And when we do so, we become something new; and although we try to hold on to the idea of who we think we are, that keeps us separate. When we surrender, we unite and become one with all things. If we don't resist, the gift surpasses anything that we can imagine. This is, I think, the key to merging into this state of Oneness: not trying to do it on our own, but allowing the transformation to be done through us.

Exercise

In the crucible of Oneness, love's all-consuming and transformational fire is fueled with your desire, devotion, heartbreak, and longing, as well as your grievances, fear, and outrage. Absolutely everything is offered to the alchemizing presence and power of Divine Love. When you fully enter into the crucible of Oneness, you become willing to receive God's healing grace, knowing that God will do for you what you cannot do for yourself.

Einstein said that you can't solve a problem at the same level of consciousness in which it was created. In the crucible of Oneness, you surrender your personal shadow sourced in fear and separation. You place it on the Divine altar and answer *yes* when asked if you're willing to be healed and transformed. This is the moment of your full surrender into Oneness, into the purifying fire of Divine Love.

Today's practice requires you to set time aside to pray for your surrender into the crucible of Oneness. You'll need at least 30 minutes. Gather your writings from Practice 21 ("The Shadow of Oneness"), as well as a candle and a bowl that's safe to use for burning. You'll also need a pen and more paper if you aren't using your journal. Create your own sacred space with these items.

Begin by relaxing your body and becoming aware of your breath. Light the candle and gaze into the warm, flickering flame. Allow its soft glow to bring you into a calm, centered, and open state. Feel the presence. Breathe in and breathe out. Notice your emotions and any bodily sensations. Bring your awareness to your heart. Feel your willingness to enter into deeper union with your true self, with God, with others, and with all of life. *Feel the presence. Breathe in and breathe out.* Pray for your wholehearted surrender; feel your longing for union increase and strengthen. Let it enfold your heart and spread throughout your body . . . permit it to infuse your entire being.

Become aware of the pain you've experienced in the illusion of separation and isolation. Feel your deep desire for release from this prison. Feel your wishes to be free. *Feel the presence. Breathe in and breathe out.* All that is required in this moment is your heartfelt surrender to the Divine. You're being asked to withdraw your investment in separation and be restored in Oneness. Become reborn and renewed in the crucible of Oneness.

Now gather your writing from the earlier practice of the shadow of Oneness. Press the pages and all that they hold to your heart. Breathe in, breathe out. Feel the presence of God as you gaze at the flame in front of you. Feel your heart open as you begin whispering the words that are rising on your lips. In the sanctity of this space, through your Soul's prayer, surrender. Give all to the All. Surrender the old life you've known, a life sourced in separation. Hold nothing back. Receive the blessings of a life lived in Oneness.

Place the pages you've been holding close to your heart in the bowl. Remain in this mind-set and now pick up your journal. Write down your prayers and statements of surrender or, if you prefer, remain in silence and stillness. (Keep your writings in the bowl on your altar. You'll return to them during the next practice.)

Continue to offer your prayers of surrender to the Divine, entering ever more deeply into the crucible of Oneness.

Affirmation

I AM surrendering myself and my life to the all-consuming, all-purifying fire of the Divine.

THE FIRE OF ONENESS

*"Spirituality is an inner fire, a mystical sustenance
that feeds our souls. The mystical journey drives us into
ourselves, to a sacred flame at our center. . . . In its presence
we are warmed and ignited. When too far from the blaze,
we are cold and spiritually lifeless. We are less than human
without that heat. Our connection to God is life itself."*

— Marianne Williamson

"The most powerful weapon on earth is the human soul on fire."

— Ferdinand Foch

*"I will set fire to the temple of your body
and make its thorns a bower of roses."*

— Rumi

James: Sometimes the only thing we can do is hold still and let the fires of transformation climb up our legs and completely consume us. We usually want to run away when it gets too hot, but this never really works. The fire follows us and appears in an infinite variety of forms, all with the intention of melting away our shadows and leading us into the light. But it's scary, for it's difficult to hold still as the powerful flames of change begin nipping at our toes. But all our impurities begin to dissolve when we finally surrender to it. We realize that the Divine fire engulfs us in Oneness and sets us free.

Anakha: In the fire of Oneness, even our attempts to pray and take part in our normal spiritual practices fall short of offering us any relief. This is what Saint John of the Cross refers to as the "dark night of the soul," where the sacred fire is doing the work deep in our Soul to purify and bring us into union with the Divine. During this stage, we may even feel like we've become detached from God. We might have reached a certain level of union with the Divine through our spiritual practice, yet all of a sudden, we find those things almost useless in the face of the holy flames. This is important because even those practices and our prayers for Oneness are consumed by the fire so they can be transformed as well.

As you mentioned, James, it requires stillness, being present to the burning. We'll feel the sweet and tender wounding of the Divine as it works on our Soul. Only the Divine physician and artistry knows how to do this; this isn't a process that we undergo with anyone else, although a therapist or spiritual director can help us navigate the dark night. It's ultimately a surrender to the fire and allowing it to do what fire does best, which is to burn away all that is no longer necessary.

James: I love the fact that you brought up Saint John of the Cross. He said that the dark night of the Soul is what brings us into spiritual maturity. It's like a child who has been held and nourished in the arms of God. When the time comes for God to set us down to stand on our own, we feel like we've been abandoned. We suddenly feel separated from God, but in reality, we're becoming stronger. We have to experience that abandonment so we can go on to the next stage, which is to realize that we're maturing into a whole new creation. This is made possible by our willingness to be consumed, and thus transformed, by the fire of Oneness.

Exercise

Today you'll enter the unifying and purifying fire of Oneness. This eternal fire burns within the inner sanctuary of your Soul and within the heart of the Divine Beloved. In the fire of Oneness, the flames become united, joining together to form a single, powerful flame. It is your Soul's deepest desire to be in union with the Divine and the Divine's desire for your Soul is no less. The only difference is that when you unite with the Divine, you become smaller and the sacred presence within you grows. You (the ego) must decrease so the I AM presence (the Soul) can increase. This is the invitation that's offered to you today—to surrender into the fire of Oneness, to be held within the crucible of Divine love and be transformed and delivered into greater union with the Beloved.

Do you have the Soul stamina to continue? You must endure the inner wounding and humbling self-knowledge so that true illumination can be received. In the fire of Oneness, the small self, the ego, is annihilated. This is the fire's work of turning coal into the brilliant diamond. This is the Divine's handiwork: burning away everything that conceals your essence so that the nature of your true self can be revealed. As 17th-century Japanese poet and samurai Mizuta Masahide wrote: "Barn's burnt down— / now / I can see the moon." This is the exposure to the workings and limitations of the false self. The fire of Oneness transforms the games and ploys of your false self and prepares you for a life of union and a consciousness stationed in Oneness.

Today's practice focuses on your willingness to be transformed by the fire of Oneness. Your intention is to cultivate an inner condition of your heart, a readiness to fully devote yourself to the embodiment of Oneness. This is your humble and life-altering vow to serve humanity by tending to the Oneness growing within you. In the flames of Oneness, you'll become an instrument of Divine joy, peace, and love. You'll receive an infusion of Divine grace as you silently sit in the stillness of the inner fire as your old self burns. There's nothing to do but call out, saying, "Beloved, bring me into union with you!" And in that simple prayer, you submit yourself to the will of the Divine. This is the hour of God, a truly joyous moment, for a thriving and sustained Oneness is the promise that will be kept. Hallelujah!

Now take the bowl with your "shadow of Oneness" writings to a safe place where you can light them on fire and allow them to burn. This is a ritual that mirrors the inner work that the Divine is enacting on your Soul. Strike a match (or use a lighter) and ignite the symbolic separation that has been placed in the sacred crucible—the bowl. Whisper this prayer: *Beloved, I surrender all of the ways that I have lived in separation. I am now ready to come into greater union with you. Burn away all that is not love, all that is not essential within me. Prepare me to serve the growing Oneness. Thank you, God. Amen.*

Watch as the fire burns the paper to ash. Feel the sacredness of this moment. When it's complete, return the ashes to the earth to nourish the soil—the Soul of a new life. Remember that this inner work—the fire of Oneness—is occurring within you. Continue to surrender all that you encounter as separation, fear, and grievance to the fire for transformation. Recite the chant: *I will, my will, Thy will.* This will serve as a prayer of devotion to union with God, the Divine Beloved.

At the start and end of your day (and as often as you feel drawn), read the Prayer of St. Francis, and know that you're being fashioned into the most perfect and wonderfully made instrument of Divine Love possible. Give thanks for this truth . . . feel gratitude for the all-consuming fire of Oneness.

Lord, make me an instrument of Thy peace;
where there is hatred, let me sow love;
where there is injury, pardon;
where there is doubt, faith;
where there is despair, hope;
where there is darkness, light;
where there is sadness, joy.
O Divine Master, grant that I may not so much seek
*   to be consoled as to console;*
to be understood, as to understand;
to be loved, as to love;
for it is in giving that we receive,
it is in pardoning that we are pardoned,
and it is in dying that we are born to Eternal Life.

Affirmation

I AM my Beloved's and my Beloved is mine,
forever united in a single flame of Divine Love.

THE RECONCILIATION OF ONENESS

"The practice of peace and reconciliation is one of the most vital and artistic of human actions."

— **Thich Nhat Hanh**

"The end is reconciliation; the end is redemption; the end is the creation of the beloved community. It is this type of spirit and this type of love that can transform opposers into friends."

— **Martin Luther King, Jr.**

"So instead of loving what you think is peace, love other [people] and love God above all. And instead of hating the people you think are warmakers, hate the appetites and the disorder in your own soul, which are the causes of war."

— **Thomas Merton**

James: Sometimes we feel the earth shake beneath our feet and believe that the world is about to come crashing down on us. But what if this is just a natural part of allowing a new world to be born through us? What if the old world is falling away, and one that operates under completely different laws is beginning to rise? When seen through this lens, the shaking and quaking takes on a higher purpose and leads us toward Oneness rather than deeper into illusion and separation.

Anakha: If we've come this far on the path of practicing One-ness, then there's something within us—what we've been calling the seeds of Oneness—that's starting to grow and affect every area of our lives. Not only our spiritual selves, but the parts we consider to be in the physical world: our finances, career, creativity, health, relationships, and so on. Everything is impacted by this newly expanded consciousness. Things start to shift, and that's when we should be saying, "Hallelujah!" and "Thank God, the process is actually working!" But it can be scary when things start to seem-ingly fall apart and fall away. We may question whether we've gone off our path or if we've made a wrong turn somewhere. Yet we can rest assured that when things do start to change, it means that there's a rewiring taking place—a profound reordering of our being and of our lives sourced in Oneness.

The mystics refer to this process as "chemicalization"—the idea that as we move to a new vibration of thought and behavior, our old belief system no longer rings true. In other words, everything that's vibrating on a plane of fear or separation will start to break down. Some of those things will completely fall away in our lives, such as certain relationships or ways of being, and some will trans-form into this new frequency of Oneness. Chemicalization is an unavoidable and crucial aspect of the embodied, spiritual journey.

James: So the question we must ask ourselves is: *What needs to be reconciled?* Is it the way we separate ourselves from our shad-ows? Perhaps it's how we hide from our light. It's like a teeter-totter that moves back and forth, up and down, until the reordering is complete. But in order to complete the process, we need to relax into the areas of imbalance, darkness, and trauma in our lives. We have to see all of it as a natural part of our evolution—an essential step of maturing into a whole new being where Oneness is fully integrated. And to do so, we need to reconcile all those diverging paths and all those seeming difficulties that make us believe that we're not enough, we're not whole, or we're not loved by God.

We must remember that God loves all aspects of ourselves, including the very imbalances we try to deny. There's nothing we need to do to deserve God's love, and if we can relax into *that* knowing, then the reconciliation takes place on its own.

Anakha: That's beautiful, and it brings to mind the experiences I've had and we've all had as humans in facing those inconsistencies in ourselves. We begin to see how we might be highly developed in the embodiment of Oneness as far as how we relate to our own health, but when it comes to relationship or money issues, for example, we might not be in that same consciousness. By entering the "crucible" and undergoing the transformation of the fire of Oneness, a reconciliation takes place in which our core self becomes unified, solidified, and rooted in Oneness. As this unfolds, we tune in to a new "frequency," which infuses and informs all the other areas of our lives and aligns them in Oneness. The sense of inconsistency and imbalance in certain areas begins to balance out so that they all start to express our essential Oneness.

Exercise

As the field of Oneness grows within you, illuminating the dark and constricted aspects of your being and consciousness, your life will begin to shake and shiver . . . shifting, changing, and growing. You'll experience a disruption in your "normal" patterns and relationships and in your own internal awareness. Your "operating system" is undergoing an upgrade to a new and improved version of Oneness, and the programs that used to run on separation will no longer work. The outward manifestation of your inward transformation will create a sacred reordering of all the areas in your life.

The consciousness of Oneness will restore you to the vibration and frequency of love, aligning your finances, work, relationships, health, creativity, and even your experience of God. The dance has changed and your partners and movements will need to change, too! This is a reconciliation of what is deepest and truest in you with what is deepest and truest in your life and with others.

Now is the time to be certain of your purpose—to serve the growing Oneness through your own transformation. As the lesser begins to break down to give way to the greater, you may become frightened or anxious. You may feel the urge to return to the illusion of safety and security that separation offered as this reconciliation begins to manifest in the outward conditions of your life. However, the door has closed behind you. You're in the transition phase, suspended between the two trapezes. Slowly breathe in and breathe out, and say, *I release the lesser to receive the greater.*

Whenever you encounter moments of fear, doubt, or uncertainty, breathe deeply and repeat the affirmation. Embrace this new awareness. Open yourself to the fresh expression and embodiment of Oneness. Remember to recite: *I will, my will, Thy will.* Know that your willingness is all that's required to allow the Divine Orchestrator to reorder your life. This is the reconciliation of Oneness at work. The past is out, the presence is now, and your future is clear.

Today, reflect on what's changing in your life. What wants to be released? What's breaking down? Do you notice anything that's shifting? How are your relationships being reordered? Your finances? Career? Health? How can you fully partner with the Divine and work creatively within this transformation? Be sure to ask yourself, *How can I be a powerful co-creator in this process of reconciliation?*

Once again, your readiness is key. Take out your journal and spend 15 minutes or so writing statements of willingness. Be sure to reflect on the following: *What new experience of the living Oneness am I ready and willing to have? What new experience of myself as an expression of the living Oneness am I ready and willing to have?*

Continue to look inward, and touch on all aspects of your life, including your health, spirituality, relationships, career, creativity, family, community, and so on.

Here are some examples of willingness statements:

I AM willing to . . .

- *. . . inspire others by being a catalyst for change in service to the growing Oneness.*

- *. . . be a grounded and devoted friend, lover, and family member.*

- *. . . serve as a passionate citizen of the beloved world community.*

- *. . . see myself as loved, desired, and needed.*

- *. . . experience my environment as vital, thriving, and creative.*

- *. . . view money as healthy, essential, and abundant.*

Now take at least five to seven of your willingness statements and transfer them onto a piece of paper or an index card. Keep it handy in your purse or pocket; or place it on your desk, dashboard, or nightstand. Recite your willingness statements throughout the day, and regard them as a powerful act of partnership between you and the Divine in the reconciliation of Oneness.

Affirmation

I AM a radiant, powerful expression of the living Oneness, manifesting love in all areas of my life.

⌒ PRACTICE 28 ⌒

THE FORGIVENESS OF ONENESS

"If we really want to love we must learn how to forgive."
— **Mother Teresa**

"The light of the world brings peace to every mind through my forgiveness."
— from ***A Course in Miracles***

"Forgiveness is choosing to love. It is the first skill of self-giving love."
— **Mahatma Gandhi**

James: We've been taught that we should forgive the wrongs that have been committed against us, but this is just the ego's attempt to be right about everything it sees and believes. In God's eyes, no sin is ever really committed, so forgiveness isn't necessary. The only thing that needs to be forgiven is the idea of forgiveness itself. Then we begin to see everything though the eyes of Oneness, and we realize the perfection that lies at the heart of every person and situation we encounter. This is no small gift—it's one that sets us free.

Anakha: As you were speaking, I found myself reaching for the middle ground between two realities. One is that (as you mentioned) in God's eyes, no sin is ever committed. So true forgiveness is when we forgive the illusion, our fearful thinking that sets us apart from the Divine. The second is that when we're thinking apart from God (when we're in the consciousness of ego or separation), there are ways in which our actions and behaviors create more division in our lives. In the forgiveness of Oneness, when we really let go of our limiting beliefs, we're able to extend this grace and compassion to others.

One way in which we can actively start to bring peace to the planet is to mend the fabric of our relationships. In other words, we can scan our past and current relationships for the moments when we may have been asleep and missed the mark, or when we didn't see with the eyes of compassion. Then we can actually make repairs so that we can experience being forgiven and healed. And we partake in this not only in a spiritual sense, but in an actual physical experience of wholeness in our relationships. This is the practice of tending to the unfinished business in our lives and in our relationships.

In an earlier practice, James, you spoke about an "access point" of Oneness. When we start to make amends and create a fabric of unity in our relationships, this is one of our access points of Oneness. This also inspires others to move into that place of forgiveness and experience Oneness.

James: *A Course in Miracles* describes this as the difference between "Level One" and "Level Two" thinking, emphasizing that we need to find a balance. Level One is the understanding that no sin has been committed; therefore, no forgiveness is required. Level Two thinking is that we believe we need forgiveness because we think we've done something wrong.

Most of all, this keeps coming back to us as individuals—the willingness to forgive ourselves and release our illusions. Then we find it much easier to offer this gift to others. So it's okay to look at both of these levels of thinking at the same time because they're occurring simultaneously. When we finally integrate all of these Oneness practices, we enter Level One awareness, which is the same as saying that we perceive the world as God does and we love one another as God loves us. I think that this is our goal: for us to enjoy this Divine *imbalance* in order to reach a harmonious place within the vision of God.

Anakha: Yes, it really makes sense to me that when we enter into the forgiveness of Oneness, it's not about forgiving a particular event or behavior. Rather, it's an extension of love. It's saying something like: "I'm sorry; I forgot who you were and who I was in the moment. Let's reconcile and get back into the relationship of who we truly are."

Exercise

Jesus asks us to forgive "7 times 70." In the forgiveness of Oneness, you're being asked to see every action and behavior as either an expression of love or a request for it, and then respond appropriately. And the only appropriate response is to offer your love and forgiveness. Extend compassion to yourself, others, and the world. In the Kingdom of Oneness, no one is excluded—everyone belongs and deserves loving-kindness.

Yes, there are natural consequences to your choices, and boundaries are set to honor your integrity. The process of forgiveness is continuous, as we receive and circulate the grace of Oneness in our lives. The ability to authentically forgive your trespasses and those of others is a demonstration of your commitment to living in the presence of Oneness.

It's time to release any bitterness or resentment and become fully available as a conduit of grace and love in the world. In today's practice, you surrender to the power of God to heal your heart, asking for Divine assistance in giving up old wounds and releasing your attachment to self-righteousness and personal justification, no matter how grievous the act. Being judgmental (of yourself and others) and holding on to past grievances block the flow of Oneness into your heart. Today, place your heart in the hands of God, and allow your Soul to lead you into the peaceful, still waters—the resting place of forgiveness.

Your ego will cling to your old habits, but your Soul will desire the sweet tenderness and mystical alchemy of forgiveness. Ask for God's help in breaking through the ego's attachment to always being on the offensive. Invoke the consciousness of Matthew 18:20: "For where two or three come together in my name, there am I with them." Invite God into your relationships, and trust that the Divine is with you, doing for you what you can't do for yourself.

Take 30 minutes today to sit in prayerful silence and reflection. Light a candle as a symbol of God's healing power and presence. Ask God to gently guide you to the places that most need forgiveness. In your journal, write down your responses to the following: What resentments have you been harboring? What amends are you being called upon to make to yourself and others? How can you heal the "mood of unlove" in your life and relationships through the power of forgiveness?

Breathe in and breathe out. Trust your guidance and the organic, mystical alchemy of forgiveness. Continue to request God's help in reconciling with yourself, with others, and with the world. Jot down the names of people you're willing to forgive. With whom are you willing to make amends? Allow yourself to be guided to the perfect healing action and communication in each circumstance. There's no right way to practice the forgiveness of Oneness. A humble and willing heart is the only requirement.

Are you willing to free yourself from the prison of separation that your resentments and judgments keep you locked in? Offer your prayers to God as you review the list of names in your journal, and wait for Divine guidance. Ask, "God, what would you have me do to heal this?" Do your part today to mend the fabric of Oneness in your life. Forgiveness is a gift—open up and receive it today!

Affirmation

I AM transforming resentments into compassion
through the power and presence of Divine Love.

⁀ PRACTICE 29 ⁀

THE HUMILITY
OF ONENESS

"Humility, that low, sweet root
From which all heavenly virtues shoot."

— Thomas Moore

"Blessed are the meek: for they shall inherit the earth."

— Matthew 5:5

"Would you become a pilgrim on the road of love? The first con-
dition is that you make yourself humble as dust and ashes."

— Ansari of Heart

James: It's easy to see that the more aligned a person is with the experience of Oneness, the more humble he or she becomes. Look at people like Mother Teresa and Gandhi—they profoundly impacted the world, perhaps more than anyone else in the 20th century, yet their humility never left them. In fact, this quality actually increased and became the source of their energy and power. They turned everything over to the Divine and were used as instruments of peace, positively changing the lives of millions of people.

What would happen if we did the same? Our accomplishments might not be as far-reaching as Gandhi's or Mother Teresa's, but we can still cultivate the humility that they enjoyed. If a humble heart actually attracts the experience of Oneness, then it may be a path worth exploring.

Anakha: We spoke earlier about the importance of *presence*. What I'm able to see in my own life is that a truly humbled presence is amazing medicine for me, for my loved ones . . . for the heart of the world. What I choose—if I'm coming from an unassuming place of service—changes my life and the lives of those around me in the most beneficial, healthy ways.

I also believe that there's a healing surrounding our mind-set that occurs the further we go into this path of Oneness. We may have been thinking that we need to be somebody other than who we authentically are in order to be of service to the world or to feel worthy and whole. Yet the further we proceed on this gracious path, the more we start to really relax into our essential nature.

The striving, posturing, and manipulation that the ego has used starts to fall away; and we're left with an open heart that's available to give and receive at any moment. The humility of Oneness is one of the sweetest, most tender fruits we're able to enjoy on this journey.

Exercise

Follow the path of modesty and reverence. The humility of Oneness softens the ego's grip on your heart and aligns you with the generosity, receptivity, and grace of the Soul. When your heart is full of humility, it becomes a home to Oneness. In this state, you offer yourself as an instrument of love in service to your brothers and sisters. Through selfless devotion and donation, an all-consuming tenderness is born and offered as the salve that heals all divisions and fuses their separate powers within you.

Humility is one of the graces of the Soul. It comes from the Latin words *humilis* and *humus* ("earth") and is related to the Greek *chamai* ("on the ground"). This quality is a way of walking, a way of being in the world; and it requires a sense of reverence for the holy ground of your Soul, the Souls of others, and the Soul of the earth. Nothing is below you other than the sacred path of Oneness. Humility invites you to walk with all people rather than separating yourself or holding yourself above others. When you enter into the humility of Oneness, you're stripped of the ego's façade of pride, arrogance, and grandiosity.

The psyche most often links humility with humiliation. This is the ego's experience of powerlessness, making you feel like your self-esteem is threatened. However, humility is a powerful and gentle aspect of the Soul. Many of the great spiritual teachers including Gandhi, Mother Teresa, Jesus, and the Dalai Lama have emphasized this trait as the doorway to liberation.

Today, spend at least 30 to 45 minutes contemplating the following questions. Write down your responses in your journal. Allow God to guide you, and be willing to hear the call for the cultivation of humility in your Soul.

1. In what areas of your life would you feel humiliation if they were stripped away? For example, your job, relationships, health, finances, physical appearance, material goods, social status, personal role, and so forth.

2. What do you fear most about being humiliated? When have you felt truly humiliated? What happened?

3. How have you humiliated yourself through your own self-betrayal?

4. Why is being humble difficult or challenging?

5. What qualities would God have you develop (from within and in your life) in order to become more humble?

6. In which areas can you demonstrate more humility? What would that look like?

7. How will you serve the growing Oneness through this practice? In other words, how will you embody and demonstrate the humility of Oneness in your life today?

Watch for opportunities to choose the humility of Oneness. Remember that nothing is below you on this journey; indeed, serve the growing Oneness with powerful acts of humility.

Affirmation

*I AM graced with humility in my Soul and
living the tenderness of Oneness in my life.*

∽ PRACTICE 30 ∽

THE ENDURANCE
OF ONENESS

"Let nothing disturb thee,
Let nothing affright thee;
All things are passing;
God never changeth."

— **St. Teresa of Avila**

"God is with those who persevere."

— from **The Koran**

"To be an artist . . . means to ripen as the tree, which
does not force its sap, but stands unshaken in the storms
of spring with no fear that summer might not follow."

— **Rainer Maria Rilke** (translated by Joan M. Burnham)

James: How much do we have to endure in order to be released from the grip of the ego and experience Oneness firsthand? How much courage does it take to remain on the path even when everything seems against us or when we feel like we're heading in the wrong direction?

These are the moments when we prove ourselves: when everything within tells us to turn back to the secure embrace of the ego. Seeing ourselves as separate and alone puts us at ease in some ways . . . until we realize how much it costs. It literally costs us everything, for the state of Oneness is sacrificed when we limit ourselves and stay "small."

This is our chance to live large and fulfill our Soul's destiny. All we have to do is endure the small sacrifices that are asked of us, realizing in the end that we didn't actually have to give up anything.

Anakha: In many ways, proceeding on this path is like training for a marathon. This is a long-haul journey. As long as we're on the planet, there's more individual and collective material to be transmuted. The further we expand into light, Oneness, and love, the more capacity we have to actually transform darkness and constriction. As sacred activists and spiritual peacemakers, part of our service is to help heal those dark and constricted places—not only in our own lives, but in the lives of others.

Through these practices, we're building endurance. Think of watching finely tuned athletes compete. It almost seems like they don't exert any effort when swimming the 100-meter freestyle or running the 400 meter. They do so with such grace and beauty because they've been engaged in this practice of endurance for a long time, and that enables them to move with such fluidness and agility.

In the same way, as we embrace our shadows and transform them through the presence of Oneness, we'll start to develop a mastery that allows us to dance in the center of Divine love. This is when we come to understand that this isn't a onetime proposition; it's a lifetime of service to the embodiment of Oneness on the planet.

James: You know, when we think about athletes and training, we sometimes hear the phrases "to feel the burn" and "to push through the pain." There comes this point where our bodies begin to ache and burn, and this is really where the gift is: overcoming that pain, enduring the burning sensation that we feel within. The same is true of our spiritual training. Sometimes we have to push through the burn and endure the discomfort because this is what builds our spiritual muscles. This is what makes us strong and teaches us compassion so that we can be of greater service to others.

Although these challenges seem to be working against us, in reality, they're our greatest allies. We're becoming more resilient so we can transform the entire planet, helping humanity ascend to its next level of evolution.

Anakha: That's a great analogy. I do believe that what stops many of our best attempts to really transform and transcend limitations is the lack of our own personal fortitude. It's that "fire in the belly" that creates discipline in this practice—even when we'd rather stay in bed, hiding out under the covers and holding on to our grievances. It's that willingness to keep going despite our resistance—to have the discipline, clarity, power, and presence to go all the way—that brings about true change in our lives.

Exercise

Facing the dark and constricted places within is a continuous spiritual practice. The journey into Oneness asks that you *bear all things, believe all things, and endure all things* in service to becoming an expression and embodiment of love. This requires courage, willingness, humility, and discipline. You must give yourself and your life over and over again to Divine love, humbly offering the ways in which you fall into forgetfulness to God. In the endurance of Oneness, your life becomes your testament to the living reality of Oneness. This is a marathon, not a short sprint! In your journey into Oneness, you'll discover endurance that you've never before experienced. Through this practice, your fear and illusion of separation become annihilated, and the brilliance of your Soul is revealed. In the words of Pierre Teilhard de Chardin: "Above all, trust in the slow work of God."

Take out your journal, and reflect on the following questions: What have you endured on your spiritual path? How has this molded or served you? In what ways have you grown? What are you learning about the endurance of Oneness? When and how do you experience the resiliency and perseverance of your Soul? How do these qualities benefit the growing Oneness?

For today's practice, spend 15 to 20 minutes outside in nature. Find a tree that you can sit or stand beside. Settle into your body and your breath. Come into communion with this beloved tree. Imagine that this living being is your guide who has been divinely selected to teach you more about the endurance of Oneness. Reach out and touch your tree. Examine its leaves and branches. What kind of bark does it have? Can you see its roots? What special markings does it have? See its beauty and magnificence; take in the details of this living expression of Oneness. Feel your connection, your Oneness, with this sacred being.

Now take a step back to view the tree from a wider perspective. Ask the tree, "What have you endured on *your* journey? What has it taken for you to grow on this earth?" Listen to its lessons of endurance. How are you similar? How have you persevered just like this tree has? Trust what you hear. Has this tree endured severe storms, droughts, or earthquakes? Has it been uprooted? Have parts of it been cut down?

Ask the tree for guidance in your own life. How can it help you with a challenge or heartbreak that you're experiencing right now? How can it fortify you with its message of perseverance? Allow it to bless you just by being in its resilient, unwavering presence. Let yourself become strong and bold like this tree, and bring the endurance of Oneness into the center of your life.

Affirmation

*I AM enduring all things in love, faithfully
living my vow to serve the growing Oneness.*

Introduction to Practices 31–40

You made it! If you're still reading, it means that you persevered through the most difficult part of the course fully intact. You know how important it is to embrace the shadow aspects of your personality in order to experience the depths of your being. You also understand that you can't go into the light until you first endure your darker corners (which we usually choose to avoid). All I can say is *well done!* Now the fun really begins.

These final ten lessons are meant to lift you up and set you on the road to Oneness. You'll notice that they embody themes that resonate deeply with the Soul, from the concept of *communion* to *vision* and many others in between. By the time you're finished, you'll be empowered to meet and transform anything the world throws at you. There are no limitations when you know that you are *One,* and that has always been the main purpose of these practices.

So take a deep breath and open your heart. You've graduated to the final phase, and you're ready to take the last step that leads to the only goal you've ever really had: *to remember the truth about who you are.*

THE COMMUNION OF ONENESS

"The human energy field embodies a collective wisdom that celebrates the divine wisdom of all. Therefore, to live in communion and union, we must embrace diversity as a brother as passionately as we embrace earth as our mother."

— **Micheal Teal**

"If we but paused for a moment to consider attentively what takes place in this Sacrament, I am sure that the thought of Christ's love for us would transform the coldness of our hearts into a fire of love and gratitude."

— **St. Angela of Foligno**

"There is a partnership, a communion between you and the land, between the land and you. This runs deep beneath the streets, deep beneath the buildings, deep throughout and beneath the seas."

— **Sharon McErlane**

James: Are we spiritual beings having a human experience or human beings having a spiritual experience? And is there really a difference? What we know for sure is that we find ourselves in this world living among and interacting with millions of other beings, yet there's also something within each of us that makes us strive for more—something we can't define that draws us into eternal spaces, beyond the limitations of the ego. At some point, we need to reconcile these experiences and realize that they're actually the same. This is what communion is all about: the reconciliation of our limited and eternal selves.

Yes, we are in a body, but no, we aren't limited to that body. It isn't who we are; it's the vehicle that helps us negotiate our way through time and space. Of course, these are all intellectual ideas, and that's not what we're after. What we really desire is the experience of Oneness, and this is where we have to begin.

Anakha: I believe that the communion of Oneness is one of the favors or consolations that the Divine grants us. It's a grace that moves through us, through our lives. Once we've completed these practices and have undergone a transformation, we begin to move in the world in an integrated way, where the mystical and real aren't polarized experiences that we have; rather they're a union, a sacred marriage deep within us. We're in a constant prayer of Oneness, and it's a relief in some ways because it can be so challenging and painful when we feel that separation . . . knowing who we are, yet often having such a radically different experience of ourselves and our lives.

When this marriage happens, we begin to feel an innate wholeness, and we realize that there's no separation. Everything is sacred, everything is holy; and the ground we're moving on, our body temples, and the Divine aren't separate at all. We are truly One!

Exercise

As a result of undergoing the purification into Oneness, every-thing is revealed as Divine. Heaven and Earth are united in the communion of Oneness—as above, so below . . . the inside as the outside, and the two into one. This is a unification of the mystical and the real. You receive your Divine inheritance, which is a radiantly awakened heart and radically embodied experience of the all-powerful presence of love. In the communion of Oneness, you're consumed by love—Lover, Beloved, and Love are one.

For today's practice, you're invited to express your gratitude for the blessing of the communion of Oneness. In the Christian tradition, the Eucharist (which means "to give thanks") is a cel-ebration of Oneness, an expression of your union with God, with your Soul, with others, and with all life. You're invited to prepare a Eucharistic meal, a sacrament to celebrate and show your grati-tude for the profound interconnectivity of life. This is the commu-nion of Oneness: God and humanity coming together, God and "flesh" . . . the flesh of wheat, wine, sunshine, soil, water, human ingenuity, stars, supernovas, galaxies, storms, fireballs.

Decide what kind of food and drink you'd like to prepare for your celebration of Oneness. You may wish to stay with tradition and choose wine and bread, or you may want to prepare milk and honey in remembrance of the Promised Land. Your meal may include a piece of fruit and sparkling water, fresh juice and choco-late, edible flowers and rose water, hot tea and biscotti, and so on. Allow yourself to freely create in ways that nourish your Soul and express your gratitude for the living Oneness.

Prepare each item mindfully, giving thanks as you bless each morsel and utensil you touch. Be fully present to the sacredness of this celebration. When your meal is ready, sit in silence and stillness. With each sip and bite, know that you're consuming *and* being consumed by the living Oneness. Give thanks for the real-ity of your deep communion with Life. Feel the sacred tremoring of the cosmos within and the wildfire of love burning inside you, and become alive in this communion of Oneness.

As you move through the day, carry this feeling with you. In other words, be in communion with all people; with nature; with animals; and with the sun, moon, and stars. Celebrate this holy union everywhere you go . . . with every step, breath, touch, and glance. Be a walking, breathing temple of communion. Know that the universe loves you unconditionally and is constantly offering itself to you in the most intimate ways. Reflect on the following passage from *Sins of the Spirit, Blessings of the Flesh* by spiritual teacher Matthew Fox, and celebrate your communion with Oneness:

> The Eucharist is heart food from the cosmos—the "mystical body of Christ" and the Cosmic Christ or Buddha nature found in all beings in the universe—to us. Christ is the light of the world, which we now know is made *only* of light. Flesh is light and light is flesh. We eat, drink, sleep, breathe, and love that light. The Eucharist is also our hearts expanding and responding generously: "Yes, we will." We will carry on the heart-work called compassion, the work of the cosmos itself.

Carry on *your* "heart-work" of love and compassion, and affirm your vow to serve the growing Oneness by saying, "Yes, I will!"

Affirmation

I AM loving life, and life is loving me in the communion of Oneness.

THE COMMUNITY OF ONENESS

"Our goal is to create a beloved community and this will require a qualitative change in our souls as well as a quantitative change in our lives."

— **Martin Luther King, Jr.**

"I am of the opinion that my life belongs to the community, and as long as I live, it is my privilege to do for it whatever I can."

— **George Bernard Shaw**

"There can be no vulnerability without risk; and there can be no community without vulnerability; and there can be no peace—ultimately no life—without community."

— **M. Scott Peck**

James: Martin Luther King, Jr., often spoke about people living together, honoring the diversity of expression, and finding creative ways to work and share that promote Oneness. He called this the "beloved community," and it's something we're still trying to realize today. The real question is: Can we achieve this in the world, or does it start somewhere deep within each of us—a decision we make in our hearts that then flows outward to others?

It's been said that we're not here to change the world, but to change our thoughts about it. What would happen if we all did that? Is it possible that our reality would begin to change on its own because the world we perceive is really just the manifestation of our thoughts? The community of Oneness is what we're evolving toward together, yet it begins by every individual making the choice within him- or herself.

Anakha: And that choice, as I understand it, is to be the presence of love, both for ourselves and for each other. It's about taking the vision that King offered us to heart: to really love and honor others in our likenesses *and* differences. I believe that the community of Oneness means that we're willing to tap into our more intimate selves, reaching out to our brothers and sisters when they stray off the path or when they need extra love and support.

We've created a world where there are so many solitary, isolated ways of living. We have our own homes, cars, and jobs; and it's easy to slip into a mode of separation. The community of Oneness is a call to open our hearts and be willing to enter the hearts of others . . . to be involved and engaged in a loving manner. Sometimes that looks like tenderness and compassion, and sometimes that shows up as a loving fierceness—calling one another to greatness, integrity, and wholeness.

James: The choice of being the presence of love is one we have to consistently make. This is ultimately what leads to Oneness: a consistent practice. We say *yes* in the moment, yet it needs to be nurtured, to grow as we live our lives. It's not something that we say in the past or the future; we must embody it right now. And we can do so in an infinite number of ways. It's not just saying the word; it's about living that action—the action of *yes*.

This demands consistency, especially when we're learning to apply this concept. The fact is that we're One right now. We're not going to "become One" someday. We're living this dream of awareness in the moment, but it's only by maintaining a consistent practice of saying *yes* that we can enter that communal experience (the community of Oneness) and be able to share it, live it, and grow within it. So I think that consistency is one of the most important elements in this whole process.

Anakha: Our commitment to "yes" is crucial as we cross the border from the metaphysical awareness and knowing of Oneness into living Oneness as our physical reality. The living Oneness permeates, infuses, and informs all areas of our lives, cutting right to the core of our relationships. Continually bringing the metaphysical reality into physical reality is a key aspect of this practice.

Exercise

The community of Oneness is the manifestation of the beloved community, where everyone is included, interconnected, and interdependent. We work together to meet the needs of all, living in global sufficiency rather than individual excess. It's a community that lives and breathes Jesus's commandment to truly and continually *love one another*. The beloved community is a living expression of the vows of oneness: to protect and care for each other and be a source of compassion and strength as we become instruments of love in service to the growing Oneness.

Your practice today is to enter the circle of love by living the vows of the community of Oneness everywhere you go and with everyone you meet. Instead of waiting for the perfect opportunity or staying in your comfort zone, perceive and receive this Divine wisdom every day. Expand your heart and exclude no one. The world community of Oneness is manifesting in the here-and-now as you practice these vows:

1. *Love others with a love that is both fierce and tender.*

2. *Watch over and care for others as you would the "pupil of your own eye."*

3. *Be a sanctuary of compassion and a source of strength for all.*

Write these vows on an index card and place them in your pocket. Or keep them where they're easily seen, such as on your mirror or refrigerator or even as the screen saver on your computer. Read them often. Make it your intention to be an instrument of love in the world by expressing these vows in all of your endeavors.

At the end of the day, take some time to contemplate and write about your experiences in your journal. What do these words mean to you? How do you practice these vows? What does it look like to love others with tenderness? With fierceness? What does it mean to care for others as an extension of yourself—that is, like "the pupil of your own eye," as stated in the Bible? How do you create a sanctuary of compassion? Are you a source of strength for others?

Finally, as you feel your own longing to return to the community of Oneness, reflect on this inspiring passage by author and activist Starhawk (from her book *Dreaming the Dark*):

> We are all longing to go home to some place we have never been—a place, half-remembered, and half-envisioned we can only catch glimpses of from time to time. Community. Somewhere, there are people to whom we can speak with passion without having the words catch in our throats. Somewhere a circle of hands will open to receive us, eyes will light up as we enter, voices will celebrate with us whenever we come into our own power. Community means strength that joins our strength to do the work that needs to be done. Arms to hold us when we falter. A circle of healing. A circle of friends. Someplace where we can be free.

Affirmation

I AM expanding my circle of love, becoming a sanctuary of compassion and a source of strength for everyone I meet.

⮌ PRACTICE 33 ⮍

THE DISCIPLESHIP
OF ONENESS

*"This world is nothing but a school of love; our relationships
with our husband or wife, with our children and parents,
with our friends and relatives are the university in which
we are meant to learn what love and devotion truly are."*

— **Swami Muktananda**

*"Nature is school-mistress, the soul the pupil;
and whatever one has taught or the other learned
has come from God—the Teacher of the teacher."*

— **Tertullian**

"Individually, we are one drop. Together, we are an ocean."

— **Ryunosuke Satoro**

James: To be a disciple means to be a student, one who learns from another person or situation. In what ways are we disciples? In other words, whom or what are we learning from? Are we following a path of love or fear? It's easy to answer this question; we just need to look around and be aware of what's manifesting in our lives.

Is your life filled with love and peace or struggle and lack? The key is not to hold any judgment—simply look at it dispassionately, knowing that you can change your course at any moment. If you're consumed by thoughts that keep you stuck in fearful patterns, have the courage to change to a different teacher today, one who promotes love and harmony. You're bound only by the decisions you make in this moment—right now. All it takes is for you to first see, then choose again, and the world itself changes.

Anakha: The awareness of what we're a disciple of and whether we are embracing what we're learning and creating in our lives is so important. In the discipleship of Oneness, everything becomes our teacher. Everything is conspiring to wake us up to the truth that we're made in the image and likeness of God, just as everything that we're seeing and experiencing in life is, as well as each person we're relating to.

We're no longer a disciple to a particular guru; rather, life itself is our teacher. The people we walk with in our day-to-day lives serve as our guides. In this practice, we observe our interactions —to what is arriving moment to moment. And instead of denying or resisting our experiences, the discipleship of Oneness invites us to look at each one and ask, *What is this trying to teach me? How can I apply this wisdom to my own life?*

James: We often seek teachers who are different from us, whether they come from a different country, practice a different religion, speak a different language, or look different from us; but what if we sought a teacher who reflects who we really are instead of who we aren't? Why not embrace the teacher who reflects our light rather than our shadow?

This is something, as you mentioned, Anakha, that we can find in every moment. All we have to do is look around and see the light of Oneness shining on us through a tree, a plant, or the smile of another person . . . to let it come to us in the most ordinary situations, in the simplest forms imaginable. We look for teachers who are different from us because we believe that we're not good enough exactly the way we are. So what would happen if we became disciples of our own higher selves, knowing that all the wisdom, all the truth we need, is already in us? Would it then expand and explode as it makes its way into the world? If we become disciples to the truth that is within, then Oneness is a natural and inevitable result.

Exercise

In the discipleship of Oneness, we consciously live the reality and truth that we are sons and daughters of a living God. We know for certain that the entire world is conspiring to wake us up to the living Oneness. We are members of the global community and express the highest manifestation of love. Through our unconditional compassion and willingness to serve one another, we're resurrected in our individual and collective wholeness. We become the holy salve—the teachers, guides, and healers as we walk the razor's edge of integrity in the practice of Oneness. We recognize each other as the face, voice, eyes, ears, and hands of God; and in our walk together, we discover the way . . . the truth that is Love.

In the discipleship of Oneness, the world is your school. Your community—friends, family members, children, co-workers, and peers—is your teacher. And your life experiences are your lessons. Your holy curriculum for the embodiment of Oneness is here now! Look at your life. What is it telling you? What is it teaching you? What new aspects of Oneness is it inviting you to explore, express, and embody? What are your challenges? Your blessings? Who or what are you having difficulty embracing as an expression of Oneness? How are you being called upon to grow? What is rising to your awareness?

For today's practice, begin your day in the consciousness of discipleship. Be willing to receive the holy curriculum of Oneness that's presented to you. Pay attention to what's persistently inviting you into greater awareness and wholeness. The universe loves you dearly and is constantly conspiring to bring you into the living consciousness of Oneness. Everything (and everyone) has been sent to awaken you, to teach you, to heal you, and to transform you. Are you willing to be a student of Oneness today? Be on the lookout for the threads of learning that when woven together make a beautiful tapestry—this is your Divine curriculum, your sacred contract . . . this is the discipleship of Oneness.

Take 20 to 30 minutes to complete the following statements. Write quickly, tapping into your stream of consciousness; don't stop or edit your words. Spend approximately two to three minutes on each statement.

- *I am being invited to heal . . .*
- *I am being invited to forgive . . .*
- *I am being invited to surrender . . .*
- *I am being invited to become . . .*
- *I am being invited to express . . .*
- *I am being invited to create . . .*
- *I am being invited to expand . . .*

Trust what you receive and what you know. Have faith in the guidance that's coming to you. Dive in, and keep it simple and clear. Cut through complexity and confusion, and discover your holy curriculum of Oneness.

Affirmations

I AM a disciple of the school of Oneness,
embracing my holy curriculum.

I AM engaging Life as my teacher.

⁜ PRACTICE 34 ⁜

THE VISION OF ONENESS

*"Great ideas, it has been said, come into the world
as gently as doves. Perhaps, then, if we listen attentively,
we shall hear, amid the uproar of empires and nations, a
faint flutter of wings, the gentle stirring of life and hope."*

— **Albert Camus**

*"Peace comes from being able to contribute the best
that we have, and all that we are, toward creating a world that
supports everyone. But it is also securing the space for others
to contribute the best that they have and all that they are."*

— **Hafsat Abiola**

*"I lived on the shady side of the road and watched my neigh-
bours' gardens across the way revelling in the sunshine. I felt
I was poor, and from door to door went with my hunger. The
more they gave me from their careless abundance the more I
became aware of my beggar's bowl. Till one morning I awoke
from my sleep at the sudden opening of my door, and you came
and asked for alms. In despair I broke the lid of my chest
open and was startled into finding my own wealth."*

— **Rabindranath Tagore**

James: Can you visualize a world where all your needs have been fully satisfied, and each person you meet is just as fulfilled as you are? It begins with the vision of Oneness.

In order to achieve this, we have to be willing to see it in our minds, perceive it in our hearts, and then allow it to come into full manifestation. If we can't visualize a world of compassion and peace, how can we hope to attain it? But we also can't stop with the vision of Oneness because it means little if we aren't willing to follow the inspiration that our mind's eye yields. Then we need to act, for God loves hands and feet that are eager to follow the prompting of the Soul. If we can see it, we can be it. All we need is the desire to manifest a new way of being in the world.

Anakha: I think that many of us would agree that we want a world that works for all, a world of peace, joy, and love. Yet many of our conflicts and experiences of separation are rooted in our fears. If we look at places where conflict and war are rampant, and we peel back the layers of concentrated separation, we find individuals who are often filled with fear just like we are. They (all of us, really) are afraid that their need for love, respect, security, or food and water—or whatever it might be—won't be met. At the core, our separation is about not trusting that there's enough for everyone—enough love, enough abundance, enough good, enough creativity, enough God, and so on. We assume a scarcity mentality, which creates conflict and separation.

In the vision of Oneness, one of the first steps we can take is to imagine a world that truly works for all—where people's most basic needs are met, and where there is no longer private, individual excess, but global sufficiency. I've heard it said many times that it isn't that we don't have enough resources to take care of the entire planet; it's that there's inadequate flow and distribution. In the vision of Oneness, we start to circulate our goods and trust the process, knowing that our needs—as well as the needs of everyone else—will be met.

James: In addition to asking, "Is there enough?" there's an even more important question: "Are *we* enough?" This is where so many of us lose our way. Individually and collectively, we don't believe that we're enough or that we're good enough. I think this is where the vision of Oneness leads us: to the understanding that who we are in our essence is more than enough. We have the wisdom; we have the light; we have the strength within. We just need to uncover what has been hidden by the fear, illusions, and perception of lack that we've given so much energy to.

But what if we began just with that thought? *I am enough right now in this moment, and my vision heals the world. The picture that I project from my holy mind is enough to transform everything I perceive.* This may sound grandiose at first, but I think it's really the opposite! It's the recognition that God's love and vision rests in each of us. And if we're willing to unleash it, then the vision of the Divine flows through us in ways that positively transform the world.

Anakha: I'm recognizing the truth you're speaking, James. If I stand in this moment and really feel and know that I'm enough, I'm contributing to the vision of "enoughness": the perception of abundance, wholeness, and wellness for the world. I imagine that when we hold the belief that says we're lacking, all of those thoughts are snowballing into a collective consciousness of "not enoughness."

Our individual part in shifting the world perception into a place where there's adequate flow and distribution—where there's enough love, food, water, and so on—starts by connecting to the Divine force where we know the truth that sets us free: *Yes, I am enough!*

Exercise

In the vision of Oneness, all of our needs are met. We feel inspired and offer our essential gifts in service to Oneness. Conflicts and differences are embraced as a doorway to the expansion of love. Every person knows who they are, where they've come from, and why they're here. This is a world where we experience a deep sense of belonging and a profound connection to Earth. The vision of Oneness is the complete embodiment of our sacred vow to *love one another*—where our attitude and actions are sourced in compassion. This is the vision of Oneness in the words of Black Elk: "The continents of the world and the people shall stand as one. We will communicate with our relatives—beast and bird—as one people. We shall know peace in everything."

Today's practice asks that you step out into the world and look upon it with awareness and discernment. Be in the world, not of it. Watch and witness. Look at the people at the grocery store, the bank, at the traffic light, at church, and at the office. Observe children, elderly people, the homeless, young adults, and middle-aged folks. Examine all of these faces; look into their eyes. How are they? How aren't they? Think about all of the unborn babies. Is this a world that will serve them? Do you think this world works for everyone?

Go outside and look at the animals, flowers, plants, and trees that live among you. Think about the rivers, lakes, oceans, valleys, and mountains. How are they? How aren't they? Is this a world that serves them? Be willing to see and feel. Be willing to cut through the veil of illusion. Pay attention to what is and isn't working. How is the vision of Oneness unfolding (or wanting to unfold) in each experience and in each person?

Now find a place to sit and be still for a while: a park bench, a busy mall, a coffee shop, a sidewalk curb. With every breath you take and with every person you see, ask yourself, *How is the vision of Oneness unfolding? Is this a world that truly works for all?* Listen and learn. Feel the truth speak to you as you look upon the world with unconditional love and compassion.

Now take out your journal and reflect on the following questions. Gently place them in your awareness, and allow the vision of Oneness to speak to you. Write down whatever responses you receive. You may wish to jot down a few words or phrases or write out longer, more detailed descriptions. Choose whatever method will serve you in your growing awareness.

1. What is God's vision of Oneness for your life and for the world?

2. How can you serve this vision?

3. How can you consciously contribute to creating a world that works for all?

4. What essential gifts and wisdom do you have to contribute?

5. Whom do you need to become to serve the growing Oneness?

6. What inspired action are you being called to take?

It's important to contemplate each question, and be patient. Open yourself to the voice of inspired guidance; and be willing to hear, see, and know the truth—right here, right now. Feel inspired and guided by the vision of Oneness today.

Affirmation

I AM serving the vision of Oneness,
co-creating a world that works for all.

ᕯ PRACTICE 35 ᕯ

THE MINISTRY
OF ONENESS

*"Your work is to discover your world and then
with all your heart give yourself to it."*

— **The Buddha**

*"To me, true service is an experience of wholeness, fulfillment,
fullness, self-reliance, and self-sufficiency for all parties—
an experience of the magnificence and infinite capacity of
human beings. When I'm really in service, I disappear."*

— **Lynne Twist**

*"Once you have found your relationship to God,
you need never look around for work."*

— **Muriel Lester**

James: When your ego hears the word *servant,* it usually thinks of someone who is less than, or subservient to, another. As with most things, the ego's vision is completely the opposite of your Soul's. Your Soul knows that by offering yourself in service to others, you're serving the world, God, and, of course, yourself. It's all intertwined, and the more you give, the more your life is filled with the riches your Soul really seeks. This is your ministry, and it's the only thing that will truly satisfy you.

Anakha: I'm thinking about the importance of this and also its simplicity. The ego loves complexity! But if we allow it, our lives can become filled with grace, ease, clarity, and devotion when we realize that we're here to be in service to Oneness. We're here to assist in the unfolding and blossoming of Oneness on the planet. And when we begin each day with that intention in our hearts and minds, we can then place our attention and energy toward its fulfillment.

It doesn't matter what interactions and experiences we have throughout the day; we're rooted in the knowledge that our sole purpose is to be a servant to Oneness, to expand the field of love and compassion everywhere we go. Everything we do is lifted into and by that vision of Oneness. And through our ministry, the expansion of Oneness is achieved.

James: The ministry of Oneness is also the "ministry of the moment." Oftentimes when I'm working with people to help them discover what their path of service is, they struggle because they think that ministry is about *doing* rather than *being.* Yet we can only be present to this moment, and this is where our real ministry lies: in looking at what's in front of us and asking, "Who can I serve right now?"

That service may be as simple as a smile or holding the door open for someone, yet we never know how much our actions impact another person's life. If someone has been on the verge of a psychological or emotional breakdown, a simple, heartfelt gesture may help him or her turn the corner. And it comes about by our willingness to be present in that moment, willing to see all people as a perfect reflection of the Divine, of Christ, or however else we wish to express it.

I think this is really the key: the ministry of Oneness is being open and aware to how we can serve at any given moment.

Anakha: I'm noticing that every time you talk about living in the moment—in the now, in presence—elation rises within me. I'm having an ecstatic experience as we're in this conversation! And throughout these practices, you and I have referred to this concept many times. I believe that we should continually emphasize that if Oneness seems far-reaching or too difficult to understand, it becomes absolutely, palpably clear and available to us when we're fully present. When we simply keep our hearts and minds focused upon the love of God and each other, then there's no grandiose action we need to take.

It's as simple as being in the moment, asking, "How do I live and expand Oneness, how do I create more love here, and how do I flow more compassion and tenderness to this person going through this experience?" And you're right, James—it can be as simple as smiling or holding a door open for someone or opening our arms in an embrace. And those seemingly small acts are actually miraculous moments that ultimately create the wave of Oneness that's sweeping across the planet.

Exercise

Today your mission is to love God and serve Oneness with your devotion to being an instrument of compassion and grace in the world. This is your creative participation in the blessed nature of God. You are a servant of the "one work"—to manifest a world that serves and benefits all. Make it your vow today to be the midwife *and* "birther" of Divinely inspired creations. Offer your services with a humble heart and in ecstatic surrender. In the ministry of Oneness, you become a flame of the life-giving fire lit up by joy, peace, love, compassion, inspiration, gnosis, and creative bliss. Act in accordance with Divine Providence for the highest good of all. This is your conscious participation in unfolding the life of God by cultivating gratitude, vision, and service.

For today's practice, remember the words of Mother Teresa: "We can do no great things, only small things with great love." The following exercises are simple and provide you with an opportunity to cultivate your ministry of Oneness . . . one moment, one prayer, and one act at a time, with great love.

Cultivating gratitude: In your journal, write down one thing that you're grateful for every day. Keep a running list. At the end of the week, create a ritual in which you read all of the items and offer your gratitude to the Divine for all of the blessings of Oneness in your life.

Cultivating vision: Spend a full minute today in loving communion with something in nature. This could be a rock, leaf, tree, cloud, wind, dirt, flower, bug, bird, and so forth. Give your complete attention, and allow yourself to fully perceive Oneness contained in this creation.

Cultivating service: Engage in one intentional, loving act of service for another person today. For example, this could include making a friendly phone call, writing a cheerful letter, preparing an extra plate of food or folding laundry for someone else, or offering a listening ear. Offer your service from a place of unconditional love, in service to the growing Oneness.

Actively share your unconditional presence and love today!

Affirmation

I AM sharing my unconditional presence and
love today, serving the ministry of Oneness.

THE KINGDOM OF ONENESS

"The whole earth is a living icon of the face of God."

— **St. John of Damascus**

*"Jesus said: If your leaders say to you 'Look!
The Kingdom is in the sky!' Then the birds will be
there before you are. If they say that the Kingdom is in
the sea, then the fish will be there before you are. Rather,
the Kingdom is within you and it is outside of you."*

— from the **Gospel of Thomas** (translated by Stevan Davies)

*"The 'kingdom of Heaven' is a condition of the heart—
not something that comes 'above the earth' or 'after death.'"*

— **Friedrich Nietzsche**

James: Jesus said that the Kingdom of God is within each one of us. What does he mean by that? Most of us were told that we have to die before we can enter Heaven, but that's not what Jesus and other great mystics taught. Oneness is in front of us in every moment—we just need to have the vision and willingness to perceive it. Heaven is also always in front of us; in fact, we don't have to die to get there—we need to *live*. It's only by really living from our Soul that we can experience Oneness and then begin to perceive Heaven right where it has always been.

Anakha: As you're speaking, I'm visualizing the generation of an "upward spiral" of love, union, connection, joy, creativity, spontaneity, and bliss. As we commit to these practices, we're creating this ever-expanding spiral of Oneness that we actually get to experience and inhabit. I do believe that this is what Jesus meant by the Kingdom of Heaven. And he said that it's within us and in our reach, closer than our own breath. It's within our conscious choosing from moment to moment whether we sow seeds of fear or seeds of love, seeds of separation or seeds of Oneness. It's really exciting to know that *yes,* indeed, the Kingdom is here now! And we can build and increase it!

I can create an upward spiral of good that not only nourishes and inspires me, but also spills over to everything that comes into my radius, my consciousness, my presence. There's a way, as we've discussed, in which we become an access point, and we also become a deep pool of Oneness that people can dive into. In the Kingdom of Oneness, our presence alone becomes a blessing.

James: I'm visualizing this spiral becoming an amazing castle-shaped edifice that represents our spiritual temple. And we're building it right now; it's not something that we'll inhabit in the future in some mysterious realm that's beyond our understanding. It's something that we have to live in now and then welcome others into. After all, who wants to live in a mansion all alone? We have to share. And as we do so, the Divine spiral that you described, Anakha, continues to move upward—it's that ascension that actually brings us into a state of Heaven. This is the Kingdom of Oneness.

Anakha: I'm guessing that this is what St. Teresa of Avila was referring to (in her work *Interior Castle*) as she described the seven mansions and seven stages of spiritual life. This path of Oneness, this Kingdom of Oneness, is a constant path, an endless spiraling staircase. It's a life of loving and creating deeper states of Oneness in our lives.

Exercise

We live in communion and radical intimacy with life. We experience Divine Love as infinite, ecstatically gathering up all things into an ever-higher and more rarified union. This is the Kingdom of Oneness—the endless upward spiral of love, joy, and peace. As citizens in this Divine Kingdom, we experience the grace that accompanies an inner harmony with our Souls that automatically creates perfect balance with life itself.

Today's practice is a moving meditation that simply invites you to perceive and receive the Kingdom of Oneness that's within you. It is above and below you. It's behind you and before you . . . to your left and to your right. Feel the truth of these words, and take a moment to fully experience this: close your eyes and bring your attention to your indwelling heart-Soul. Breathe life into this sacred place. Feel the presence. Feel the power. Know the beauty it holds. Whisper these words to your heart: "The Kingdom is within me, the Kingdom of Oneness is within me, the Kingdom of Heaven is within me, the Kingdom of God is within me, the Kingdom of love is within me." Breathe in, breathe out, and sink ever-more deeply into the Divine Kingdom that lives within you.

Once you've fully connected internally, open your eyes and look around. Feel the Kingdom within you as you see the Kingdom outside of you. Whisper these words: "The Kingdom is within me, the Kingdom is outside of me, the Kingdom surrounds and enfolds me." Continue with the regular tasks of your day, remaining in the "Kingdom consciousness." Perceive and receive all that is above, below, behind, before, to the left, and to the right as the Kingdom of Oneness. With everyone you meet, silently say, *I am you and you are me.*

Look upon everything and everyone as a member of the Kingdom of Oneness. Notice when this challenges you and when it's easy to do. When you encounter a difficulty or feel strained, ask the Divine to dissolve your separation and fill your mind with love and compassion. Become willing! Continue this practice for the entire day, immersing yourself in the Kingdom consciousness as you attend to others and the activities and events that make up your day. With each breath, step, and prayer, you're advancing closer to Oneness.

At the end of your day, take out your journal and reflect on the following questions as a demonstration of your commitment to living in Oneness, now and always.

1. What are your Divine responsibilities as a citizen in the Kingdom of Oneness?

2. How can you cultivate the Kingdom consciousness within you?

3. In what ways can you be a fruitful lover of God and messenger of Heaven in your life?

4. How will you create an upward spiral of joy and love in the Kingdom of Oneness?

Affirmation

I AM living in the Kingdom of Oneness—above, below, behind, before, to the left, and to the right—I AM, I AM, I AM!

⌒ PRACTICE 37 ⌒

THE INTIMACY
OF ONENESS

*"When fear dissolves, you no longer separate yourself
from this single flow of immense force. Love is continuity
with infinite life force, a Oneness of being with no separation.
[Love is the key to] opening to this flow of life force."*

— **David Deida**

*"The value of the personal relationship to all things
is that it creates intimacy . . . and intimacy creates
understanding . . . and understanding creates love."*

— **Anaïs Nin**

*"Long seeking it through others,
I was far from reaching it.
Now I go by myself;
I meet it everywhere."*

— **Tōzan** (translated by Katsuki Sekida)

James: Almost everyone has intimacy issues. Some of us have learned how to overcome our fear of being close to another person, yet many of us barely sense the fear that rises within when someone really *sees* us. What is it we're afraid they'll see if we open ourselves to love? Are we afraid they'll notice our shadows, our faults? Or is it just that it's sometimes hard to love ourselves without conditions, to give ourselves the intimacy that we so desire from others?

By now you may realize that this is a gift you have to give yourself before you can receive it from another person. But when you do allow your heart to open to the love that's always present within, it flows easily and naturally. If you hold it back from yourself, how can you hope to be intimate with a lover, a friend, or anyone else? The intimacy of love is what you've really been looking for all along—you just have to be willing to open wide and receive it.

Anakha: I think this brings us to the question of how much love, joy, and connection we're willing and able to experience. Oftentimes, we've created a glass ceiling for ourselves, a box to live in. And even when great love comes knocking, we resist it. I'm recalling what Marianne Williamson says: that it's our light, not our darkness, that we're most afraid of. When we open to intimacy, it's true that others will see our shadow, yet they'll also witness our brilliance and creativity and all of our other aspects of Oneness that live within us. They'll actually perceive the Oneness shining in us and as us. When we resist, we do this partly out the fear of our own Divine nature. Eventually, as we're able to relax and trust ourselves, our brilliance, our light, intimacy becomes a beautiful and nourishing exchange.

I recently gave a spiritual-direction session with a young man who is very intelligent and gifted spiritually. He shared that when he was just a sixth grader in Catholic school, a nun pulled him aside and said: "You are special. You are brilliant, and you need to be a role model." In that moment, he got the idea that to be brilliant, he was going to have to "do" something. Yet at that young age (and having just lost his father as a result of divorce), this little boy was already overwhelmed with the responsibility of being the "man of the house." He didn't want to have to "do" anything more. When we uncovered and released his limiting belief, he was able to experience the brilliance of Oneness, and let his light shine.

In the intimacy of Oneness, we invite each other to show up in the light and to just be in love and brilliant together, which can be an exhilarating, yet also terrifying, experience.

James: A few years ago, I directed a film called *Into Me See,* which, of course, is about intimacy. I love the title because it reveals that it's not about anyone else; it's about seeing into *me,* my own heart. Once I do so, I'm able to begin the work that's required to enter this state of love first with myself and then with others.

To enter the intimacy of Oneness, I have to turn inward, revealing my deepest thoughts, my innermost desires. If I can do that, then being intimate with others will be easy because I have in many ways already welcomed them into the deepest parts of who I am. In my heart, I can make a home for anyone. It doesn't matter if it's a lover, a friend, or a stranger I meet on the street; I can make a home for each person who comes into my presence because I've embraced the Oneness that we share.

Anakha: That's true, and I also think that in the intimacy of Oneness, part of the alchemy between ourselves and others— whether it be a romantic relationship, a close friendship, or a spiritual experience within a community—is that we're required to grow into our own wholeness, our own embodied Oneness. Oftentimes, our resistance to intimacy is also our resistance to evolving in profound ways. It's a resistance to our own wholeness and Oneness. The invitation that this practice offers us is to come into a relationship and be willing to call forth the best in each other and also the places where we need to heal and grow.

Exercise

The intimacy of Oneness is a sacred and holy place. It is the I-Thou relationship with all life, a living Namaste—perceiving, receiving, and honoring the Divine light in one another. When we're humbled in our humanity and glorified in our divinity, we become infused with the realization: *I am in you, you are in me, and ours is a most sacred union.* We simultaneously experience the ultimate vulnerability and ecstatic blessing of Oneness. We expand our knowing of ourselves and of one another. We experience the love and desire that the universe has for us and the attraction and allure we have for it. We share an ever-more intimate dance in the Kingdom of Oneness. We make love to each moment through our uninhibited expression of the Oneness that is. We become the beloved, the lover, the consort, and the companion. This is the romance of our lifetime: the love affair with the living, waking, breathing God. This is the intimacy of Oneness.

Today you're invited to explore the rapture and radiance of being alive. This is the moment—right now—for your full surrender to love. This is your solemn vow: to be a radical lover in the world and to live in the intimacy of Oneness. Moment to moment, you choose whether to wake up or remain asleep—don't be a dead fish in the ocean of God.

Approach your day without holding back: Choose to live and love with an unguarded heart. Before you rise in the morning, take a moment to pause and connect with your heart. Feel your heartbeat. Feel your breath as you watch your chest rise and fall. Feel your body, your flesh, your bones. Feel the blood coursing through your veins. Experience the sacred intimacy you have with your own magnificent self. What are you sensing? What are you thinking about? What are you wanting? Tune in to your internal awareness.

As you get ready in the morning, move slowly, maintaining a graceful connection with your breath, body, and actions. As you shower, feel your skin, muscles, and bones. Be present with your own Divine temple. Allow yourself to touch and be touched with the items around you: a smooth bar of soap, a plush towel, a silky tie, worn denim jeans, soft cashmere socks. Feel the sensations of intimacy all around you.

As you glance in the mirror, look into your eyes. What do you see? Breathe in and breathe out. Take in the image of Oneness that meets you in the mirror. Give yourself time to become fully present in this moment. Feel your own Divine human presence. Whisper "I love you" as you gaze at yourself. Feel the depth of your connection to your Soul. Breathe in and breathe out. Experience all of the emotions that accompany this intimacy. Are you touched and grateful or resistant and critical? Just notice everything without judgment or analysis.

Continue with your day; and practice being intimate with everything you touch, taste, hear, see, and smell. Commune with an orange, tango with a flagpole, soar with an eagle, whistle with a bird, coo with a baby . . . permit yourself to explore the realm of radical intimacy. Be a fool for the sake of intimacy! Become fully available—"naked" and vulnerable—to life. Embrace all that arrives to greet you, and be alive and joyful.

Now extend this intimacy to those around you. Be willing to experience others as they truly are. Look beyond the masks, the roles that people play. See into the heart of another, and be open to the life force that exists between you. Feel the I AM presence move you into greater awareness and ever-more fulfilling experiences of the intimacy of Oneness.

Take out your journal, and spend about 30 minutes reflecting on the following questions as a demonstration of your devotion to embracing the intimacy of Oneness:

1. How can I create more intimacy with myself, with God, with others, and with life? What small yet powerful steps can I take?

2. What would loving with an "unguarded heart" look like in my life?

3. How can I calm my fears and soften my heart so that I'm more available to the intimacy of Oneness?

4. How can I move into a more vulnerable and open experience of intimacy with others?

5. What do I need to release? What should I embrace?

6. How would living in the intimacy of Oneness bless me? Bless others?

7. Finish this statement: "The intimacy of Oneness I long for is . . . "

While you're lying in bed tonight, say a prayer. Ask the Divine Beloved to work with your heart and Soul as you sleep, delivering you to the Promised Land, the intimacy of Oneness.

Affirmation

I AM waking up, experiencing the ecstatic nourishment and the radical intimacy of Oneness in life.

THE PRAYER OF ONENESS

"I always begin my prayer in silence, for it is in the silence of the heart that God speaks."

— **Mother Teresa**

"Pray without ceasing."

— **1 Thessalonians 5:17**

"The man whose prayer is so pure that he never asks God for anything does not know who God is, and does not know who he is himself: for he does not know his own need of God."

— **Thomas Merton**

James: The Desert Fathers taught their disciples to "pray without ceasing." This philosophy forces you to look a little deeper at prayer and discover how it leads to Oneness. Imagine a telephone conversation: you may not always be speaking, but the awareness that you aren't alone, that there really is someone else you can be present with, keeps the energy alive. It also stimulates a deeper level of intimacy. This is the essence of the prayer of unity—the awareness that you're always communicating with life, with love, and with God. This leads you to a more meaningful experience of Oneness.

Anakha: As I was reflecting on these practices yesterday, I was sitting outdoors on a porch swing here in Portland, Oregon. It was 58 degrees and warm for February, and I could sense the prayers of nature all around me: I could hear the birds singing, feel the sun's rays on my face, and touch the dead and dying leaves and barren tree branches. It was as if all of Creation was engaging with me in this prayer of Oneness.

Even on a busy street in downtown Seattle or in the middle of Times Square in New York City, there are unceasing prayers all around us that we can open to and let move us. As I was listening to the birds' sweet song, I had the sense that they were affirming: *Yes, this is the way. Yes, love is the way.*

James: What you're describing sounds very Franciscan to me. This is something that St. Francis of Assisi really lived. He wrote prayers about Brother Sun, Sister Moon, Brother Sky, the wind, the fire, the rain . . . and he was within all of these natural elements, to the point that he was one with them. There are stories of him preaching to the birds and conversing with a wolf. All of these beings that we think of as wild, St. Francis was able to "tame" because he knew that "wild" part within himself. He achieved this through prayer, understanding that we're always communicating with life and with God.

So I think if we can just maintain the awareness—and it doesn't mean that we're constantly praying words—then we'll experience a state of Divine presence in every moment. And this is the most important, most effective prayer we can be living on a daily basis.

Anakha: Yes, the prayer of Oneness (unceasing prayer) and the communion of Oneness are tightly intertwined. As we're seeing, all of the practices feed each other and flow together. There's a dynamic upward spiral that's starting to occur as they're consistently engaged, and the prayer of Oneness brings them all together.

Exercise

You are a living prayer of Oneness. Your entire being is sacred medicine—the "manna" for others. You live in communion and pray without ceasing. You are a channel of love and grace in the world.

Today's practice has three parts. The first part invites you to be in constant conversation with God everywhere you are and everywhere you go. Engage in this dialogue just as you would with a dear friend, which God *is*. Place your awareness on the presence of God, and feel yourself naturally drawn into an ever-flowing conversation. Make the Divine your constant companion. How does practicing the presence of God transform you? Your life?

The second part of this practice asks you to become an embodiment of prayer: a living, breathing, walking, talking, eating, sleeping prayer. Your prayerful presence is all that's necessary to achieve this. Make everything you do a prayer by devoting all of your actions (and inactions) to serving the growing Oneness. Remember that you're standing on holy ground—the "ground" of your own being—right where you are in this very moment. Fan the flames of love, the Divine spark within you, and become a living prayer of Oneness. Allow this prayer by St. Teresa of Avila to inspire you:

Christ has no body now, but yours.
No hands, no feet on earth, but yours.
Yours are the eyes through which Christ looks compassion
    into the world.
Yours are the feet with which Christ walks to do good.
Yours are the hands with which Christ blesses the world.

The final part of today's practice involves becoming aware of the unspoken prayer that lives in the center of your heart. In the words of author and spiritual teacher Dr. Matthew Robertson: "There is a prayer that lives in the center of your heart. If you pray it, it will change your life. How does it begin?" What is the prayer that lives within your heart that when uttered will change your life?

At the end of the day, sit in silence and loving communion with God. Breathe and become still and centered. Enter the temple of your heart. Listen to the sound of your unique inner drumbeat. There's a prayer waiting to be heard. What is it? Allow yourself to speak it freely now. This is your prayer of Oneness.

Affirmation

I AM a living prayer of Oneness in constant
communion with God and all life.

⮜ PRACTICE 39 ⮞

THE JOURNEY OF ONENESS

"The feeling remains that God is on the journey, too."

— St. Teresa of Avila

"The great and rare mystics of the past . . . were, in fact, ahead of their time, and are still ahead of ours. In other words, they most definitely are <u>not</u> figures of the past. They are figures of the future."

— Ken Wilber

"When you wake up to the Divine Consciousness within you and your divine identity, you wake up simultaneously to the Divine Consciousness appearing as all other beings. And this is not poetry and this is not a feeling, this is a direct experience of the divine light living in and as all other beings. And until this realization is firm in you, you do not know who or where you are."

— Andrew Harvey

James: Too often we're consumed by thoughts about our final destination or our goals in life that we miss the small miracles along the way. In a spiritual sense, many of us have been told that our purpose is to achieve enlightenment, so we focus on that and do whatever it takes to get there. But what if enlightenment isn't the absolute goal? What if it's the *journey* to realizing our sacred self? In other words, perhaps being a spiritual person and experiencing Oneness is really about relaxing and enjoying the fruits of every moment.

Anakha: Seeking something outside of ourselves, even in a spiritual context, keeps us out of the presence of Oneness, focused on striving and achieving. A limiting belief such as "I'm not enough as I am right now" prevents us from tapping into the truth of our wholeness and well-being. And yes, the journey into Oneness is like a flower that blossoms and then dies and returns to the earth, and then grows once again and repeats the cycle. It's this continuous flowering that the journey of Oneness invites us into. It calls us to embrace and savor all the phases of the growth process, whether we're in the darkness of the soil in the cold of winter or in the full and magnificent bloom of springtime.

All of these experiences of expanding Oneness in our lives must be embraced because each one grows out of the other.

James: *A Course in Miracles* describes the "journey without distance." I think this is what the journey of Oneness is all about. We're on this path, yet it doesn't seem to ultimately lead us anywhere, except where we are right now. I mean that we're already in Heaven; we're already enlightened; we're already whole. We may, for a moment, perceive that we're somewhere else, or that we're in some other state of being. And yet, when we enter the journey of Oneness, it's really about realizing who we are and where we are right now—as we take each step and put one foot in front of the other.

Once again, the more present I can be on the journey, the more that this realization enters into me: I can clearly see that I never left my source. I'm home! I'm already in the Heaven that I seek. This is, I think, the greatest understanding: we don't really go anywhere, but we still have to take the journey to come to that realization.

Anakha: There's a beautiful polarity that we get to hold in this: there's nowhere to go, yet we're always arriving into a new state of Oneness. Yes, we're in an unfolding process, and we're whole and complete just as we are. And yes . . . there's more expansion of this consciousness to live and experience in our lives, and it's all here right now. It's one of those "both/and" realizations. I think when we discover a polarity like this, we also find the deep truth in it. To hold both of those ideas and experiences simultaneously is part of what the journey requires.

Exercise

This is a journey to the Infinite—there's no ending or beginning. When we find ourselves arriving at one station of Oneness, it is but a start to another endless and boundless journey into ever higher, greater, and more embodied states of Oneness. We're brought into the dimension of infinite transformation and transfiguration. This is the voyage of God becoming God in and through all of creation.

This practice leads you to recognize the paradox of the journey into Oneness. It is the awesome, holy, and sometimes baffling place of "both/and." In other words, you are Divine and you are becoming Divine. You are One and you are becoming One. You are whole and you are becoming whole. There's nowhere to go and everywhere to go. The journey is now and the journey is infinite. We are home and we are going home. What happens when you hold these seemingly opposing ideas as aspects of the One essential truth?

For today's practice, meditate and reflect on the following passage from the Song of Songs 2:13:

The fig tree has ripened its figs,
And the vines in blossom have given forth their fragrance.
Arise, my darling, my beautiful one,
And come away!

Hallelujah! *Yes,* you've ripened on your journey into Oneness. You're being called to continue . . . *to arise and come away!* As you spiral into Oneness, you'll discover that you can always rise higher; there are greater states of Oneness to embody. Saint Gregory of Nyssa said: "The divine course is never exhausted. We must therefore constantly arouse ourselves and never stop drawing closer and closer in our course. For as often as He says *Arise* and *Come,* He gives us the power to rise and make progress."

Spend about 30 minutes reflecting and praying about the following questions. Write your responses in your journal. Embrace and celebrate the "both/and" aspects of your Divine journey into Oneness.

1. How has Oneness ripened within you and your life?

2. How has Oneness blossomed in your relationships?

3. What fragrance is being released in and through your presence?

4. What are the qualities—the fruits of your journey into Oneness—that are being expressed in your life?

5. How will you celebrate your journey into Oneness thus far?

6. What new aspect of your journey is being initiated?

7. What is calling you to "arise and come"?

8. In what areas of your life can you further express the consciousness of Oneness? For example, relate this to your relationships, your career, your health, your finances, your creativity, and your sexuality.

You may also wish to experiment by drawing spirals in your journal or making Möbius strips as symbols to activate meditations on your journey of Oneness.

Affirmation

I AM transforming from glory to glory, becoming that which I already am, birthing divinity in my Soul.

☙ PRACTICE 40 ❧

THE MYSTERY OF ONENESS

"Do not now look for the answers. They cannot now be given to you because you could not live them. It is a question of experiencing everything. At present you need to <u>live</u> the question. Perhaps you will gradually, without even noticing it, find yourself experiencing the answer, some distant day."

— **Rainer Maria Rilke** (translated by Joan M. Burnham)

"All that I have seen teaches me to trust the Creator for all I have not seen."

— **Ralph Waldo Emerson**

"The mystery of God holds you in its all-encompassing arms."

— **Hildegard of Bingen**

James: Oneness can seem very mysterious, at least from our perspective. We normally see everything through the lens of our mind (our personality) or even through our body. It's no surprise, then, that we're far more comfortable with separation than unity. But when the shift occurs, when we align with the vision of our Soul rather than our ego, what once seemed mysterious suddenly becomes obvious and crystal clear. Then we realize that Oneness isn't a mystery at all; it's the most certain thing in the universe.

This has been the goal of these practices from the beginning: to make that shift and then to consciously live in it. It's time for us to see the simple truth, for when we do so, Oneness becomes a state we can live in consistently.

Anakha: I love this! It's another polarity, too: it's simple and it's here right now, yet it *is* a mystery. We can conceive the idea of Oneness and receive it right now; but we can also taste it more fully, deepen it, or experience it in expanded ways. This reminds me that there are natural stages of development, both spiritually and mentally, just like as we journey from a small child to an adult. Through these practices, having experienced them myself, I can feel how my embodiment—my lived experience—of Oneness is growing. What I didn't know yesterday about Oneness, each day I find that I'm learning and experiencing more and more. The mystery of Oneness inspires childlike wonder and makes us say, "Wow, the Oneness that I'm experiencing right now is amazing! What could possibly surpass this that I don't even know about or can conceive of yet?"

As God is birthing God through us and through our individual and collective experience of embodied Oneness, we sense that, in a way, God is a mystery to God. In other words, we are the seeds that the Divine has planted, but whom are we going to become as we blossom into our fullness? This mystery draws us to a place of curiosity and awe—this open, childlike experience of Oneness.

James: There's nothing wrong with being entertained, and sometimes we entertain ourselves better than anyone else ever can. I think this is what this practice is all about. We make it mysterious because it keeps us engaged, and that's a very good thing. Being engaged in life is also a very good thing. If it were boring, we'd quickly lose interest. So it's almost as if we keep a part of reality cloaked, just beyond our reach, so that the intriguing enigma continues to pull us along, closer to the experience of Oneness.

Yes, we are already One. We are already whole and enlightened. But this mystery we've designed is really so grand and beautiful because it gives life a quality that we might not otherwise have, which allows us to be fresh and keep the Divine flow active everywhere we look.

Anakha: I think the mystery invites us into a dynamic relationship with life and vitality. The tantric tradition has a sacred text called the Spandakarika, which means the "sacred tremoring." In the mystery of Oneness, we're alive with this sacred tremoring as well as with all creation. As we enhance our own experience of Oneness, we're expanding Oneness throughout the universe. We're in a dynamic, co-created partnership of the embodiment and expression of Oneness as we live these practices in every moment in our lives.

Exercise

Today you'll take communion with the ultimate mystery—the holy place, the "cave within the heart"—where you simultaneously experience the center of the universe and your Soul. This is the mystery of Oneness: your direct, unmediated marriage with the Divine and your intuitive knowing of the transcendent, imminent Presence. Through your impassioned devotion and discipline to the 40 practices, you've reconnected the radiant heart of Oneness to the living mystic within you. You've been consummated in the love of God and immersed in its mysteries. You're invited to step into your essential nature: a skilled practitioner in the art of establishing, embodying, and expressing a conscious connection with the mystery of Oneness.

There have been many names attributed to the Great Mystery. Mystics, saints, and sages throughout time have described it in their poetry, music, art, and writing. Reflect for a moment on the following names. Which ones resonate with your wise inner knowing? What do you call the mystery of Oneness?

- The Hidden Heaven
- The Eternal
- Radiant Darkness
- Holy Nothingness
- The Numinous
- The Tremendous Mystery
- The Unknown Unknowable
- The Cloud of Unknowing
- The Inconceivable
- The Kingdom
- The I Am Beyond I AM

- The Luminous
- The Holy
- The Veiled Face of God
- The Way
- The Cosmic Mystery
- The Great Ultimate
- The Vast All-Encompassing
- The Magnificent
- The One
- The Alpha and The Omega

Today's practice invites you to experience your unique connection to the divinity contained in all things. This requires you to rid your mind of old images and concepts, and experience the mystery of life from a beginner's perspective, free from limitations and past associations. This clears the way for you to have a direct encounter with "a nothing and a nowhere" that will lead directly to the unfathomable experience of God. You need to become like a child again: open, curious, innocent, and available.

Today's practice takes you out of your day-to-day surroundings and into the natural world in order to partake in the mystery of Oneness. Nature is one of your most powerful access points to the mind-blowing, awe-inspiring mystery of God. Ponder this as you experience God's holy creation. Observe and appreciate the unknown that's contained and infused in all things. Allow your fixed perceptions to dissolve, and see with the eyes of love and compassion. Look upon everything with wonder and awe. Experience life as if it were brand-new. See, hear, taste, touch, and smell for the first time. Behold the vast sacredness that surrounds you, and enter the awesome mystery of the universe.

Plan your excursion into what Matthew Fox calls the "primal sacraments": the sea, land, wind, fire, life, and the universe itself. Whether you spend 30 minutes or an entire day in nature is up to you. Create an experience that will honor your inner mystic and nourish your Soul's longing for intimate communion with Oneness. What aspect or area of nature is drawing you to it? Where will you go to enter the "cave of your heart"? It's been said that St. Francis of Assisi often sought out caves to pray in. Where will you take refuge to pray with the mystery of Oneness?

As you spend time in nature, revel and marvel at the mystery. Be receptive to all that's holy, and fall in love with the universe, with all of creation. Be enraptured. Allow yourself to shudder, tremble, and tremor with the awesome mystery of life. Feel, sense, be, and come alive! Breathe in the life and love around you. Feel the universe loving you as you love the universe; enter this intimate relationship with wild abandon and complete surrender. Become intensely attracted to and immensely allured by all that surrounds you. Allow the mystery to enter you. Experience God flowing into you, as captured by C. S. Lewis: "Something of God . . . flows into us from the blue of the sky, the taste of honey, the delicious embrace of water whether cold or hot, and even from sleep itself."

Be fascinated. Perceive the luminous mystery. Allow your Soul to gaze upon the mystery without any veils. As Yeshua said: "Know what is in front of your face and what is hidden from you will be disclosed. For there is nothing hidden that will not be revealed." Allow the mystery of Oneness to be revealed to you.

At the end of your day, take time to reflect and write about your experience in your journal. Like the mystics who have come before you, consider expressing your direct encounter and perception of the mystery of Oneness with words, songs, symbols, movements, stories, and art.

Affirmations

I AM part of God's vast and holy creation,
one indivisible, Divine mind.

I AM the mystery of oneness unfolding.

⇜ PART II ⇝

ACHIEVING THE IMPOSSIBLE

By now you've hopefully watched my short film *The Proof,* where a young woman hides a book somewhere in the continental United States, and just by having her focus on the exact spot, I'm able to find it. (If you haven't seen it yet, I encourage you to go to **www.jamestwyman.com**, and click on the link for *The Proof.*) Part II of the course is meant to teach you the fundamentals of this skill so you'll be able to accomplish the same task. Sound impossible? If you begin with that kind of attitude, it probably will be . . . but if you're confident and have an open mind, you'll be amazed by how easily this is accomplished. You'll be able to re-create my experiment, and although you may not choose to use the entire country to test your skills, the result will be the same: you'll have tapped into the stream of Oneness. You'll become a miracle worker.

Does it surprise you to know that I never tried finding an object hidden in such a large area before I shot the film? Let me provide you with some more background information. As I've mentioned, I'd already mastered the technique many years earlier, or at least the first level, but the idea of hiding an object anywhere in the country never occurred to me. I'd heard stories of people who had accomplished this feat within a city or town, but no one—at least to my knowledge—had ever attempted something so enormous. I decided to practice first: I placed an ad on **Craigslist.com** to recruit assistants who would hide small objects at the local mall. They could conceal the items wherever they wanted—in a shoe at the shoe store, under a pile of sheets at the department store, and so on.

It wasn't until I remembered a line from my favorite book, *A Course in Miracles,* that I even considered attempting my experiment using the entire country. It said: "There is no degree of difficulty in miracles." In other words, a big miracle operates according to the same laws as a small one. If I could find a spoon hidden inside a shoe at the mall, then why not a book hidden in a bush in Seattle? I decided that there was very little difference, and from that moment on, I had complete confidence in my ultimate success.

However, from the beginning, there was one primary concern that nearly made me abandon the project altogether. It wasn't that I was concerned about whether or not I'd be able to accomplish it. The issue was more about what might happen afterward. Society tends to put so much focus and importance on things that appear extraordinary, psychic, or paranormal. As I'm writing this, in fact, I'm aware of at least four television programs that are dedicated to mediumship, extrasensory perception, and a wide variety of other interesting psychic skills. Did I want to be included in this group? For the last 15 years, my work has involved promoting peace and performing as a musician all over the world even while wars raged around me. I'd even decided to fulfill a dream I had since I was very young: to reenter the Franciscan order and become a friar.

What a strange departure *this* would be, and it was hard to tell where it might end.

But my own curiosity ended up getting the best of me. Although I was confident in the way I would ultimately accomplish the task that lay before me, there was still a seed of doubt—a question I had to answer for myself. Could I really achieve something that had never been done, and if I did, could I use it in some way to teach a deeper lesson—something that would significantly impact millions of people around the world?

And that's why I'm writing this course. If my only goal was to impress people, I would have stopped with the movie. But the fact that *I* was able to find the hidden book means that *all* of us possess this skill. If we can tap into it, it may lead us toward more meaningful aspects of our lives that have been ignored until now. What if finding the book was exactly what I needed to inspire people to dive inside their own selves and unleash the energy that's capable of transforming their lives, their communities, and the entire world? It may sound like a tall order, but it's what I believe in my heart.

So how does this relate to the 40 Practices? Well, once you realize that you have the power to create miracles (like finding a hidden object with only the power of your intuition), you'll want to go deeper into the recesses of your Soul in order to experience Oneness consistently. Just as in the practices, consistency is key because a momentary flash of insight will do little to positively affect your life. I encourage you to go back and forth between the two sections of this book, giving yourself the opportunity to explore these different states of consciousness.

That being said, you're about to embark on a journey. In these next few lessons, you'll learn the skills you need to find an object that's been hidden by someone. I'll show you how to tap into an internal sense you may not have known you had. But that's just the beginning! Once you achieve this, you'll hopefully, as I did, learn to apply it to many other areas of your life, developing a sensitivity that will allow you to work miracles wherever you go.

You'll be aware of the flow of energy and insight that's all around you in every moment. What if you were able to be more attuned to people so that you're available to them in deeper, more intimate ways? After all, if you can work a small miracle—like finding a hidden object using your intuition—imagine what the possibilities could be.

THE SENSE OF TOUCH

Have you ever experienced what you'd call *Oneness?* Perhaps in a moment of contemplation you felt intimately connected with everything around you. Or maybe you were deeply in love, and the walls and separating boundaries that would normally seem so inescapable suddenly crumbled at your feet. It could have even taken place during a time that would have otherwise felt totally normal or ordinary. Think back and see if there's a reference point, something that gives you the sense of what this course is all about. Now ask yourself, *Do I want to experience this—and more—in every moment of my life?*

This is the reason why you were born: to experience Oneness all the time, knowing that you are One with everything around you. And then to take it even one step further . . . you're here to experience yourself as One with whatever concept you hold of God. That's the goal of this course. It's not only about learning how to read someone's mind, but to consistently experience what the mystics and saints have described throughout the ages as the culmination of being fully human: the ability to know that you are One with everything you perceive.

Let me stop for just a moment because there's something I want to make sure you don't miss. You may wonder what I meant when I said "whatever concept you hold of God." It's obvious that many people have different ideas and experiences of God, depending on their personal beliefs or how they were raised. In addition, there are those who have no concept of or belief in the Divine at all. The question then becomes whether having such a concept is necessary in order to learn how to tap into another person's thoughts (as I did in my film). Or to go even further, is it necessary to believe in order to access a much wider range of impressions often referred to as psychic or paranormal?

I'll make it easy on you and say that as long as you accept that there's something beyond your limited range of experience (that is, the things you can experience through normal sensory input), you'll be fine. One person may call it God or Allah, while another may simply refer to it as the Universe. Suffice it to say, on your own you're limited, but there are ways of transcending those limitations to experience other realms of possibility.

Here's another way of understanding this concept. Imagine that you're a computer with a finite amount of memory and processing speed. Even if you were very powerful, you'd still be limited in how much work you're able to do at a given moment. Now imagine that you hook up to the Internet. Everything suddenly changes because—although the same limitations apply—you have a dramatically expanded field of opportunity. You now have access to information from millions of other computers around the world, sharing ideas, programs, pictures, and sounds that you didn't have access to on your own. You're still who you are, a single computer, but you're also One with the flow of data from every other computer on the planet.

This is what we mean by Oneness.

Now that you have a better idea about what the word means, it may be helpful to jump right into the experience. Here's what I hope to accomplish in this first lesson: You'll be able to experience the first level of connection with another person so that when he or she hides an object in your home (or wherever else you are), you'll be able to find it simply by having the individual focus on its location.

Imagine that for a moment. In *The Proof* movie, you witnessed me successfully locate a book that had been hidden in the continental U.S. You may not be able to expand your horizon quite that far—at least not at first—but I guarantee that if you follow these instructions and keep an open mind, you'll be able to accomplish that same feat. What you're about to learn is that Oneness can be felt in many ways and on many levels. Once you've mastered the beginning stage, you'll be able to expand on what you've learned and experience it consistently throughout your life.

Are you ready?

That question may seem very simple, but I promise that it's much more significant than you can imagine. Realizing that you're genuinely ready is of ultimate value. If you read this material and then say to yourself, *There's no way I can accomplish something like that,* then that's exactly what will happen. But if you begin right now by affirming: *I AM ready to experience Oneness on profound new levels and accomplish what would have before seemed miraculous,* then you'll be amazed by the results. It's all up to you.

There's one more thing I want to say about this process and the course that you're reading now. Learning to find a hidden object simply by having a person concentrate on its location may seem like a dramatic effect, but it's just the tip of the iceberg. In some ways, it's nothing more than the bait that hooked you, convincing you to look a little deeper than you normally would. But if you're willing to suspend your critical mind and have faith, you'll be surprised by how far you can go. This first lesson puts you on the path to finding a hidden object, but what I really hope is that you'll find yourself, your own hidden power. When you do, miracles will begin unfolding all around you, and you'll achieve every dream you can imagine.

That being said, let's get started. The first steps allow you to realize how much you can discover from your sense of touch.

The First Steps

Take a small object, whatever you choose, and have someone you know hide it in a specific room or anywhere in your house. (You may want to start with a small area and work your way up, but you'll soon discover—as I did when I had the whole country to work with—that the size of the area makes very little difference. Once you attune yourself to another person, finding an object in a large building will be no more difficult than a single room.) Now have the individual stand in front of you and ask her to focus on the precise spot where the object is hidden. (I'm picking *she* to avoid the awkward "him or her" construction. Of course, this lesson applies equally to males and females.) She should visualize the place as clearly as possible, even feel the object with her fingers as if she were standing right in front of it. The more senses involved, the clearer the signal will ultimately become.

Now have your friend open her eyes and take hold of your wrist, squeezing with normal pressure. Explain that she should simply walk behind or beside you and not say a word. Her only job is to direct you to the spot *in her mind.* In other words, she'll have thoughts such as: *To the left . . . stop here . . . it's lower . . . that's it!* The more energy she puts behind her mental instructions, the easier it will be for you to pick up the signals. So begin to walk (have your friend continue gently holding your wrist), hesitantly at first, but you'll soon start to hear a distinct inner conversation taking place that offers you guidance. Within seconds or minutes, you'll realize that you've arrived at the spot, but now you'll need to zero in. Move your free hand back and forth until you feel the impulse to *stop.* When you're certain you're there, look around. You'll probably spot the hidden object or sense that it's behind something directly in front of you. Once you can do this, you've accomplished the first level.

Examining the Roots of the Method

In order to be successful, I'll break down the process I just described in more detail and also provide the history behind the technique. You're going to be amazed by how simple this is and how easy it is to accomplish. And yet, it's really just the first step, the most introductory level of experiencing Oneness. It opens the door, allowing you to see that there's so much more than what you commonly perceive, a whole new world beyond the limitations of the five senses.

As I mentioned in the beginning of this book, in the early 1900s, a magician named Alex Hellstrom developed a "trick" that has intrigued people ever since. I don't know if he realized the enormous implications of his discovery, but it became the stepping-stone that allows us to enter this new world. His technique became known as *Hellstromism,* or "muscle reading," and it relies on a mentalist's (a mind reader, one who's extremely perceptive) ability to read a person's subtle physical reactions to various events. Hellstrom's theory was that our unconscious mind reveals what we're thinking through involuntary physical reactions, and by interpreting those reactions correctly, a mentalist is able to get a glimpse into what we're actually thinking.

What I really want to stress, though, is that this is *not* what I'm referring to when I talk about tapping into Oneness. However, it's a step in the right direction, and by experiencing it for yourself, you'll be able to take the next, and far more important, steps.

Throughout the movie, I had very minimal contact with Leslie (she was my volunteer who agreed to hide the book somewhere in the continental U.S.). But at the beginning of the film, you may remember that I asked four volunteers to hide items at a grocery store. While pinpointing each object's location, I held a pen and had the person who hid the item hold the opposite end of it. This was to prevent me from gaining cues through the individual's muscles or physical reactions. My goal wasn't to test my skills in Hellstromism. I've been performing this technique for many years (since I was a child), and I've discovered that through constant practice, there's a level of communication that has nothing to do with Hellstromism. In this place, this state of consciousness, the walls of separation fall away, and you simply *know* where the object is. This is the state of mind I wanted to show in my film and teach you now.

Remember that in the end, however, it has nothing to do with finding a hidden object—your mission is to apply this knowledge to the ordinary moments of your life. When you achieve this, then you'll understand just how far you've come.

Before you can do that, you'll need to get a general sense of how to read a person's involuntary muscular reactions. After a little practice, you'll be able to accomplish this with relative ease, and then you'll be ready to experience a deeper connection that will be described in the next two lessons.

Let's go back to the beginning: The first step is to ask a friend to hide whatever kind of object you decide on. It doesn't matter what it is, but make sure that once it's chosen, it doesn't change. There are also a couple of rules you need to explain to your "assistant" before she embarks on her expedition. First, she must hide the object in a place you can actually get to. If she puts it in a locked safe, there's little chance you'll be able to succeed since you probably don't have superhuman powers. The second rule is that the hiding place must be stationary. (I once asked someone to hide an object but forgot to explain this rule. My friend hid the item in her pocket. I walked around in circles completely confused until I realized what I'd done. You don't want to repeat this mistake!)

Most important, your friend must *want* you to find it. If her real goal is to trip you up by thinking about one spot when it's really hidden in another, you're going to head to the place she's thinking—not where it's actually hidden. Explain that she needs to literally scream the instructions in her mind in order for you to receive them. The more focused she is, the easier it will be for you to pick up the subtle impulses and find the object. In addition, it's crucial that she doesn't say or do anything other than walk beside you. At this stage, she's just going to hold on to your wrist (applying average pressure) and give you directions mentally.

Here's an example of what your explanation may sound like:

"Now that you've hidden the object, I want you to close your eyes and imagine the spot as clearly as you can. Visualize every detail—reach out in your mind's eye and touch the object so you know how it feels.

"Open your eyes and take my wrist. Hold on with a normal amount of pressure. In a few seconds, we're going to start walking, and all I want you to do is walk next to me and tell me in your mind how to get to the spot. Of course, don't say anything out loud, just think the directions, such as: *Go forward . . . now to the left . . . you went too far, go back . . . you're here, stop now!*

"It's also important that you really scream the thoughts in your mind, and you have to actually want me to get there. If you try to trick me, you'll succeed, but if you follow my instructions, we'll probably walk straight to it."

You're ready to begin! Take one step forward, then stop. You may feel the person step forward very naturally, a possible sign that you're heading in the right direction. If you feel any resistance, it may be an indication that the object is in the opposite direction. Pick one way and start walking. Don't go too slow because your partner will be less likely to give you strong signals. It's best to move fast, even a little jerky. The natural tendency will be for your friend to pull or push you in the right direction. Once again, this will be very subtle, but it will be there if you concentrate, and your friend won't know that you're "reading" her in this way.

Keep walking until you feel the impulse to stop or change direction. This urge may come in several different ways: you may feel an actual physical sensation (a pull or tug that tells you where to go), or you may even sense something deeper (a knowing that has nothing to do with your friend's physical responses). If you sense the latter, you're way ahead of the game. For most, this won't happen right away, so continue to be open to the impulses that come to you through your friend's hand or direction of her body.

I usually find that given the right "subject," I can walk to the object without any hesitation, almost as if she's telling me in actual words how to get there. The method you saw in the movie with Leslie isn't something I can repeat with just anyone. It takes those who have a very high degree of skill projecting their thoughts for me to find the object without any physical contact, but it can be done consistently once you've opened yourself to these lessons. If you practice and attune yourself to this mind-set, you'll also find that this is a lot easier than you think.

There will come a point when you *know* you've arrived at the spot. How will you know? You'll feel certain because your subject won't let you walk away. Literally. As long as she's focused and really wants you to find it, she'll actually pull you back to the spot if you try to walk away from it. Of course, she won't realize this because her muscular reactions are so subtle, but you'll feel it. Once you're confident that you're in the correct spot, it's time to zero in.

Ask your friend to (mentally) guide your hand to the precise spot where the object is hidden. You'll begin by putting your hand near the floor and asking her to think *stop* when your hand is at the right height. You may need to go up and down a bit, but like before, you'll feel a definite sensation to stop when you're there. When you have the right height, move your hand from left to right, and repeat the process with your friend. Wait for the sensation even if you have to go back several times. If you're having a lot of difficulty, ask her to really concentrate and scream the instructions into your brain. If you're able to find the correct location, you should be able to see it at this point or know that you have to move something over to get to it. Perhaps you're in the kitchen and there's a box of cereal in front of you, which tells you that the object is most likely directly behind the box. Be patient and trust yourself. You can do this! If you believe that this is easy, it will be; and your friend will be completely astonished when you reach forward and pull out the hidden object.

Now that you've learned the basic technique, it's time to practice. You may discover that you're a natural and can find hidden objects with little effort. You may, on the other hand, have a very different experience and notice that you spend a lot of time walking in circles. Don't give up. As I said, this is something almost anyone can do, and once it's achieved, you'll have crossed the first threshold.

After more practice, you're ready to move to the next level—finding the hidden object with *minimal* physical contact. This is the point where your intuition begins to take over, and your experience will be very different from your initial attempts. Until now, you've relied almost entirely on muscle reading, the subtle physical reactions of your partner. This is a good trick, but it's only a trick. As I've said, the main goal isn't to impress your friends; it's to open your consciousness to a new level of communication, one that's unfamiliar yet feels very natural. When this door has been opened, you won't ever let it close again.

Now is the time to clarify your intention. Ask yourself, *Do I intend to go all the way and realize on a very deep level that I am One with every person and situation?* If you said *yes,* then keep going! This first lesson was only an introduction—a first step that offers the slightest hint of what's possible.

In the next lesson, you'll discover that there's a whole language beneath the common speech that fills most of your days. In fact, you're always communicating in this unseen, often unconscious manner, even more than you do with words. I'll show you how to become aware of this language and then teach you how to converse in it. When you do so, you'll discover a new world opening right before your eyes.

THE LANGUAGE
BENEATH ALL LANGUAGE

Human beings put infallible faith in the words they speak to others and the words that are spoken to them. We began learning this when we were young, long before we could speak the words that would enable us to interact with the people in our lives. At first we heard sounds come from their mouths, and their faces seemed to indicate that there was some meaning that we were missing. Eventually, we were able to interpret many of these sounds and make sense of them, but we still couldn't return with words of our own. After a couple of years, though, we were finally able to complete the cycle and use simple phrases and sentences to express our thoughts, hopes, and concerns. We had learned to talk.

But as much as we gained from this, a great deal was also lost. When we were very young, our communication took the form of feelings and intuition, and we were able to judge what was occurring around us from a very deep perspective. This is because the words weren't in the way, and we learned to perceive situations directly instead of through a series of interpretations.

What do I mean by this? If you think about it, words are really symbols of symbols (as *A Course in Miracles* says); therefore, they're twice removed from the truth. An experience begins with a direct perception. For example, let's take the perception of rain as it falls to the ground. At this point, without language, I'm in the direct experience of this moment, but in order to really understand it, I need to develop a concept that allows me to wrap my mind around what I'm perceiving.

This is the second level—the concept, which, as you might have already guessed, isn't based on what's happening right now, but what has occurred in the past. I ask myself, *When did I feel a similar sensation, and how was this different from the rest?* Before long, I'm able to gather enough evidence that allows me to form a mental construction (in this case, "rain that falls on the ground"), and because of this, I'm able to devise a word. *Wet!* Now I'm able to "language" what I had previously only understood in symbols, but in doing so, I've removed myself from the actual experience.

I don't know what anything is for!

Here's an experiment you can try. Look around and choose something to focus on. It could be a chair, a pen, or even a picture on the wall. Usually, you'd look at one of these things and say deep within your subconscious mind: *This is a pen because it looks similar to other pens that I've seen in the past, that I've felt in my hand, and that I've written with on paper. I know this isn't a pencil because it writes with ink instead of lead. If I'm not careful, that pen can break, and if it's in my pocket, it will stain my pants because it happened to me once when I was ten.* On and on this process goes, all in the span of about a tenth of a second. Of course, you aren't aware of any of it. You simply look at the object on the table and think: *pen.*

But what would happen if you had no past association with it? Would you have any idea what it is, or would you immediately search through the archives of your mind to find the thing it comes closest to? But what if nothing came close to what you're perceiving? What if you didn't have anything to compare it to?

**You would perceive it directly—
not through the filters of the past.**

Look at the object you've chosen and release all concepts you hold about what it is or what it's for. Look at it as if it were for the first time and say within: *I don't know what this is for.* Allow it to tell you what it is. Maybe you'll pick it up and roll it through your fingers. Imagine that you're from another planet, and you're looking at this thing with no previous experience. Let your imagination run wild, with no preconceived ideas or concepts . . . just your intuition. When you feel the task is complete, pick another object and do the same. Follow this pattern until you have a tangible experience of what lies beneath all your ideas and concepts—come face-to-face with the thing itself.

Animals don't rely on words to speak but on the "language that lies beneath all language." They're able to communicate with each other through instinctual responses and can therefore access a tremendous amount of information that would seem invisible to the average human. A wolf raises its nose in the air and knows that a deer is a mile away. The deer also senses that it's in danger and decides whether it should respond or wait for more information. Nature teaches us to perceive all things as a direct experience, while words are like boxes that contain and limit our experience, removing our original, organic perceptions.

This is what you want to regain, and it's essential if you want to move to the next level of practicing Oneness. In the first lesson, you learned how to find a hidden object by relying on the subtle reactions of someone with whom you maintain a physical connection. If you're to begin moving away from sensing these things physically and begin perceiving them on a heightened plane, you'll need to release your need for concepts and words, trusting instead the infinite amount of information that lies *behind* them.

Walking Exercise

Choose a busy location where you can walk among other people—a crowded mall or a busy street, for example. Take a few deep breaths and relax as much as possible. You won't need to say a word to anyone—in fact, this is the whole idea of the exercise, beginning the process of sensing the information that lies behind the words we usually cling to.

When you feel like you're ready, start walking through the crowd and pay close attention to your feelings, not your thoughts. Don't walk around with thoughts such as: *That woman seems nice, but the guy she's with looks like a jerk.* This is what limits your perception. Simply feel your way through the people, opening to the rush of emotions and sensations. You many want to stop now and then to relax or center yourself. Do this as long as you can, knowing that there's no specific goal except to detach from your words and concepts. It's time to trust your feelings, for this is what will lead you to experiencing Oneness on a much deeper level.

Making Minimal Physical Contact

In the first level of this program, you learned how to become sensitive to the physical reactions of a person as they guided you to the spot where they hid a given object. You were probably surprised that you were able to sense these reactions—just as shocked as your partner would be if you told her that she was projecting her thoughts to you. Every thought we think has a corresponding physical reaction that's impossible to hide. For example, there's a great television show called *Lie to Me* about highly trained professionals who are able to observe people's physical cues to determine whether or not they're telling the truth. One of the things they look for are micromovements, which are instantaneous facial expressions that may only last a tenth of a second but reveal a person's genuine feelings. Now that you're becoming more accustomed to these subtleties, you'll be surprised by how much more you can pick up.

The next step in the process of experiencing yourself as One with another person is to begin relying less and less on those physical cues. You'll recall from *The Proof* movie, when we were in the grocery store looking for the hidden spoons, I had each woman hold on to the opposite side of a pen as we walked between the aisles together. At that point, I was no longer able to sense their pulse, any subtle changes in temperature, or whether or not they squeezed my hand. And yet, there were still some physical changes I could sense, like the tiniest tug in one direction or another. This forced me to open my consciousness wider to welcome in the emotions and feelings that might guide me to the spot.

What emotions and feelings could I be referring to? You may have noticed that when you were practicing the first level, you may have occasionally felt a strong impulse to move in one direction or another; and then a second later, you felt your helper give you a physical cue that confirmed your inner knowing. You received the cue emotionally before you received it physically.

Unfortunately, at the time you weren't able to trust that feeling, so you probably disregarded it. From this point on, however, you'll begin relying on your feelings and emotions rather than any physical reactions from your partner.

Going Deeper

Ask your helper to hide an object just like before. The first steps in this method will be the same as you've been previously practicing. None of the rules are different. The only thing that changes is that instead of your partner holding on to your wrist, she'll hold on to the end of a pen or pencil, and you'll grasp the other end as you walk together (this is just like the process you saw me demonstrate at the grocery store in the film). Try to get a sense of movement once she's taken it. Move your arms back and forth a bit so you can sense how much tension is normal. This will help you sense when your partner is adding more than a normal amount of pressure.

As you begin to walk, pay close attention to any physical stiffness or rigidity from your partner. It may indicate that you've gone the wrong way or passed the spot. Be receptive to anything your partner is unconsciously trying to communicate. But now is when you must also combine this with a close examination of the feelings and emotions you're sensing. You may suddenly *feel* that you should turn left. Follow your instinct and compare it to what you sense from the pen you're both holding. There will also come a point when you simply know that you're close. Watch body language, being aware as you were in the first stage when you were relying completely on physical reactions. But now it's time to trust your instincts, knowing that you're indeed connected to your partner on a deeper level, capable of tapping into their mental instructions.

Remember that you're watching for the *language that lies beneath all language.* There's a level of communication taking place every moment of your life that you aren't consciously aware of, but like any animal, you can follow and predict it if you tune in to inner awareness. It's vital that you trust you can do this. It will definitely take more time to master this stage than the first level, but with perseverance, you'll enjoy much success. Then you'll be ready for the final step: *no physical contact!*

⌒ LESSON THREE ⌒

THE FINAL STEP

Is it possible to combine everything you've learned so far—from the 40 practices for embodying Oneness to the techniques for tapping into the thoughts of others—and take the final step into a new world? It may be easier than you think; in fact, it may be the most natural thing you've ever done . . . if you would only believe.

You've been told that you're alone, isolated from everything you perceive. A short inquiry might reveal that you've always had the ability to dissolve the illusion of separation and experience the intimate thoughts of others. Most people brush these experiences off as coincidence or chance encounters. The next time it happens, stop and pay attention. Is it possible that you proved Oneness on your own a very long time ago?

The 40-day program outlined in this book is a logical approach to a very illogical premise. All the lessons, whether the 40-day process or the instructions for finding a hidden object, serve an important purpose, giving you a template to place your experiences in. When you accomplished the first level of finding an object while physically touching another person, you realized that there's a profound connection between the thoughts you think and your body. Then in the second level, you observed that you could begin removing yourself from the physical connection and use a conduit (in this case, a pen) to accomplish the same thing. But now you're about to take a step beyond both of these . . . a step into the mystery itself.

No physical contact!

It's been said that Oneness isn't something that can be described in words but only realized through direct experience. The same applies to this final step. Until now, I've given you techniques for tapping into the thoughts of other people, both through their physical reactions as well as the impulses you feel when you're with them. Once you break all physical contact and simply have your helper walk beside you, all bets are off. The fact is that you already have all the tools you need. Now it's time to act.

In my experience, I'm able to successfully find hidden objects without having any contact around 40 percent of the time. (With physical contact, either direct or indirect, my rate of success is around 95 percent.) This is extremely high and comes from years of experience. If you're able to accomplish the same results 10 or 20 percent of the time, you're doing extremely well. Don't worry about how often you can do it, but focus on how much more attuned you become to the subtle movements of energy in your life. The goal, after all, is not how well you can find hidden objects, but how the practice helps you experience Oneness itself.

You'll remember that in the movie, I asked Leslie to walk beside me but not to say a word. It's possible that having her in close proximity had little effect on my success, but it did make me feel more relaxed; and being relaxed, of course, is of extreme importance. Experiment with it for yourself, and see how you feel. Having Leslie walk next to me, however, did offer some clues as to whether I was moving in the right direction. I may have been walking one way but sensed tension in her steps. It may or may not have been something I saw with my eyes—oftentimes, it was something I felt.

Trust this feeling if you sense it. Then test it. Turn around and walk in the opposite direction, and see if your partner feels more relaxed. If she does, it may mean that you've made a proper choice. Once again, this is about tuning yourself to a frequency, and once you've found it, you'll know.

A good way to practice this is to repeat the walking exercise from the previous lesson, with an added twist. Walk through a crowded street and observe the people who are walking toward you. They may be several yards away, but if you watch them and really pay attention, you'll usually be able to predict whether they intend to walk to the left or right of you when they pass by. You'll possibly even sense this with your emotions before they give off a physical cue that indicates their intention. This is a good way to build up your confidence and learn to trust your instincts.

Another exercise is to stand with a person you know and simply look into her eyes. Ask her to imagine a scene from the past— something that happened that left a strong impression. Perhaps it's the first time she kissed a person she was falling in love with or when she gave birth to her child. It's important that she recounts a story that deeply affected her because the stronger the emotions it produces, the easier and more clearly she'll project them to you.

As she visualizes the scene, look into her eyes and be aware of any feelings that come up. Don't concern yourself with actually *seeing* anything. That will come later. For now, it's the emotion you want to sense—the images will eventually follow. After a moment or two, relate what you picked up to your partner. If what you sense is close, use that as a point of reference to zero in more clearly. In other words, if you feel joy and she confirms that feeling, then you can eliminate thoughts of fear or sadness. Stay with the joy and let it deepen, relating the emotions as they come to you. If you told your partner that you're feeling a sense of dread, and she says you're off the mark, release that and go in a new direction. It may take time before you're able to identify the actual emotional state that she's in at a particular moment, but if you practice, you'll be amazed by how quickly it will come.

Be creative and see if you can come up with your own experiments. The main thing to keep in mind is that this is natural—you do it every day but usually aren't conscious that it's happening.

If you start bringing more focus to the exercises, you'll begin to know what it feels like to tune in to others, and you'll recognize the impressions they create in you. You'll be able to slip in and out of this mind-set effortlessly.

I personally find that when walking beside someone who has hidden an object, I can often walk to the general spot without any physical contact. Zeroing in can be a different story, though. If the person is a particularly good sender, there's a good chance I'll still succeed. If not, then I may have a pen in my pocket that I can resort to, using it to pinpoint the exact spot. This won't distract too much from the final effect. The fact that you're able to follow your emotions as well as the cues to arrive at the right location is a miracle itself. Using a pen or even having your partner hold your wrist at the very end doesn't mean you failed.

As I wrote earlier, the most important thing you can do is to try it for yourself. The rules you learned in the first two levels still apply. Now you just need to find a willing partner. Of course, it's vital that your partners focus their thoughts as powerfully as they can. If there was ever a time you needed some energy and help, this is it.

☞ AFTERWORD ☜

What has been gained from this course? Perhaps you bought this book because you saw the short film *The Proof* online, and you wanted to learn how to find hidden objects using the power of your intuition. If that was your goal, then you most likely achieved it. But is that what you really wanted? Is that why your Soul led you to this book? Perhaps you discovered this on the shelf of your local bookstore, and the idea of a 40-day program for experiencing Oneness appealed to you. You may have had a concept of what Oneness is, but now that you've gone through all the practices and exercises, something new has happened. It's no longer an idea in your mind, but a reality you can enjoy and share. In either case, whether you bought this to come closer to Oneness or to develop your psychic skills, you end up in the same place, with the very same question that must be answered: *What now?*

How will this impact you? How will it help you experience life in deeper, more fulfilling ways? And most important, how will it help you achieve the longing of your Soul—the longing you've felt from the time you were born that you're just beginning to activate? Will these lessons remain concepts that you file somewhere in the deep recesses of your brain, offering occasional insights when you feel lost and alone? Or will you use them to transform your life, to step into a whole new way of being, activating the power that has always been within but has been asleep and inactive until now? Simply put, will you take this seriously and let it be the foundation of a life that has a powerful affect on a world that desperately needs inspiration? Now that you have this information, the choice is yours.

Years ago, I offered an Internet class called "The Spoonbenders Course." The idea was that you could take the simple lessons and learn how to bend a spoon with your mind—something that was made famous by the Israeli psychic Uri Geller back in the 1970s. More than 60,000 people took that course, largely because the concept was so unbelievable. Who wouldn't want to possess such a skill? Imagine being able to go to a party and demonstrate such an amazing feat!

What my students didn't know, at first, was that the spoon-bending part of the course was really just a hook. There was a whole other reason for engaging in the lessons. From the e-mails I received, I'd say that roughly 25 percent were able to successfully bend a spoon with their thoughts to some degree. At the same time, though, I didn't receive many unhappy e-mails, maybe 10 or 12 in all. That's because people realized very quickly that the real goal was to understand the operation of miracles—to achieve a *miracle mindedness*.

Most people experienced miracles in their lives that weren't originally desired or intended, and they attributed it to the lessons they learned through the course. In the end, whether successful at bending spoons or not, the majority realized that if all of us could see the real lesson, we'd be a step closer to bending the whole world toward peace.

The concept behind *The Proof* is very similar. When I had the idea of trying to find a book that a volunteer had hidden for me somewhere in the U.S., I knew that it would attract a great deal of attention, just as the Spoonbender Course did. But I also knew that I wouldn't be able to teach such important lessons without first sparking people's interest.

Whether or not you can find a hidden object has no real value in the end, but your ability to experience the Oneness that's all around you in every moment *does*. That's why this book focuses on the practices much more than the psychic phenomenon. Hopefully, you've noticed that and were able to ride this powerful wave all the way to the Promised Land.

I know I speak for Anakha when I say how transformative this process has been for both of us. We had to live it to engage in the dialogue that produced the heart of this book. We had to dive into the center of each of these practices and experience them on the deepest levels possible, and we're both better people for it.

I hope that you'll go back to them again and again, as I'm sure I will. This book is meant to be lived, not just read. I trust that you'll continue to grow and experience Oneness in profound new ways, and in doing so, you'll transform your life and the whole world. That, after all, is why you're here . . . you already have the proof.

In peace,
James F. Twyman

☙ ABOUT THE AUTHORS ☙

James F. Twyman is the best-selling author of numerous books, including *The Moses Code, Emissary of Light,* and *The Art of Spiritual Peacemaking.* He's also an internationally renowned "Peace Troubadour" who has a reputation for drawing millions of people together in prayer to positively influence crises throughout the world. He has been invited by leaders of countries such as Iraq, Northern Ireland, South Africa, Bosnia, Croatia, and Serbia to perform The Peace Concert—often while conflicts raged in those areas; and he has performed at the United Nations, the Pentagon, and more. James is the executive producer and co-writer of the feature film *Indigo,* and the director of *Indigo Evolution* and the documentary *The Moses Code.* He is also a member of the Order of St. Francis and the co-director of the World Community of Saint Francis.

Websites: **www.themosescode.com** and
www.jamestwyman.com

Anakha Coman is a sacred-heart mystic walking and teaching the path of embodied love and reclaiming the sacred feminine. She is an ordained New Thought minister and founder of The FireHeart Sanctuary (**www.fireheartsanctuary.com**), a beloved community of sacred activists devoted to resurrecting the essential teachings of Yeshua and Magdalene and living the Christ consciousness.

Following the events of September 11, Anakha left her career as a successful executive in the high-tech industry to answer the call to ministry and service. This led her to work as a spiritual counselor, healing intuitive, and facilitator ministering to individuals, groups, and incarcerated women. She has devoted her life to living the true mystic's path, inspired by those who have come before her and guided by Yeshua's clarion call to love one another.

Anakha holds master's degrees in divinity and applied behavioral science, as well as postgraduate certificates in expressive-arts therapy and spirituality, health, and medicine. She is an inspired speaker who shares her intimate experience of the mystic's path with churches, spiritual centers, and organizations throughout the Pacific Northwest and abroad. Her personal spiritual practice includes ecstatic dance, Kundalini yoga, unceasing prayer, quiet contemplation, mystical erotic poetry, raw foods, and an abundance of dark chocolate.

Her Website, blog, and video teachings can be found at: **www .naked-heart.com.**

~ NOTES ~

NOTES

NOTES

NOTES

NOTES

NOTES

NOTES

NOTES

NOTES

NOTES

⁓ NOTES ⁓

~ NOTES ~

NOTES